CONTENTS

Feminist Review is published three times a year by a collective based in London.

The Collective: Avtar Brah, Ann Phoenix, Annie Whitehead, Catherine Hall, Dot Griffiths, Gail Lewis, Helen Crowley, Nel Druce, Sue O'Sullivan.

Corresponding editors: Kum-Kum Bhavnani (USA);
AnnMarie Wolpe (South Africa).

Correspondence and advertising
Contributions, books for review and editorial correspondence should be sent to:
Feminist Review, 52 Featherstone Street, Londone EC1Y 8RT.
For advertising please write to:
Journals Advertising, Routledge, 11 New Fetter Lane, London EC4P 4EE.
Tel: 44 (0)171 583 9855; Fax 44 (0)171 842 2298; E-mail jadvertising@routledge.com

Subscriptions
Please contact Routledge Subscriptions Department, Cheriton House, North Way, Andover, Hants SP10 5BE. Tel: 44 (0)1264 342713; Fax 44 (0)1264 342807;
for sample copy requests, e-mail sample.journals@routledge.com; for subscription and general information, e-mail info.journals@routledge.com. A full listing of Routledge books and journals is available by accessing http://www.routledge.com/routledge.html

Notes for Contributors
Authors should submit four copies of their work to: *Feminist Review*, 52 Featherstone Street, London EC1Y 8RT. We assume that you will keep a copy of your work. Submission of work to *Feminist Review* will be taken to imply that it is original, unpublished work, which is not under consideration for publication elsewhere. All work is subject to a system of anonymous peer review. All work is refereed by at least two external (non-Collective) referees.

Bookshop distribution in the USA
Routledge, 29 West 35th Street, New York, NY10001, USA.

Typeset by Type Study, Scarborough
Printed in Great Britain
by Bell & Bain Ltd, Glasgow

ISSN 0141-7789

The *Feminist Review* office has moved.
Please send all correspondence to:
Feminist Review
52 Featherstone Street
London EC1Y 8RT

In Love with *Inspector Morse*:
Feminist Subculture and Quality Television

Lyn Thomas

FEMINIST REVIEW NO 51, AUTUMN 1995, pp. 1–25

Abstract

This article consists of textual analysis of a highly successful television series, *Inspector Morse*, combined with qualitative audience study. The study of *Morse* and the fan culture surrounding it is presented in the context of a discussion of recent feminist work on the texts and audiences of popular culture. The textual analysis focuses on those elements of the programmes which contribute to its success as 'quality' television, and particularly on *Morse* as an example of the role played by nostalgic representations of Englishness in 'quality' media texts of the 1980s. The article goes on to discuss whether the presence of such representations in these programmes leads inevitably to a convergence of 'quality' and conservative ideology. The discussion of the ideological subtexts of the programmes then focuses on the area of gender representation, and on the extent to which feminist influences are discernible in this example of quality popular culture, particularly in its representations of masculinity. The second part of the article presents an analysis of a discussion group involving fans of the series, which was organized as part of a larger qualitative study of the fan culture surrounding the programmes. There is a detailed discussion of the impact of the social dynamics of the group on their readings of *Morse*. The analysis also focuses on the ways in which the discourses identified in the textual analysis, such as gender representation, quality and Englishness, are mobilized in talk about the programmes. Finally, the nature of the group made it possible to discuss the construction of a feminist subcultural identity in talk about a mainstream media text, and to identify irony and critical distance as key components of that identity, particularly in the discussion of the pleasures offered by the romance narratives of the programmes.

Keywords

feminism; audiences; television; Englishness; identity; masculinity

Introduction

Inspector Morse (Zenith, 1987–93), a conventional crime fiction series with two male heroes, may seem an unlikely starting point for a discussion of feminism, but it is precisely this apparent incompatibility which renders *Morse* a suitable vehicle for the exploration of the relationship between feminism and contemporary British popular culture. *Morse*, perhaps more than any other television series, has become synonymous both with quality and mass popularity; if *Morse* can represent the often contradictory obsessions with economic success and high cultural value of the new Conservative era, then in this study they are juxtaposed with a social movement often regarded as having little to contribute in either sphere, relegated to a cultural Jurassic Park. This juxtaposition poses questions about the nature of subcultures and their relation to more dominant cultural forms generally, and about the extent to which, in the late 1980s and early 1990s, feminism can be seen as incorporated in the mainstream or surviving in the margins. Here these questions arise in the context of analysis of a popular television programme and of some aspects of the fan culture surrounding it. My approach combines analysis both of the text, and of a group discussion taken from a larger study of *Morse* fans. This article is part of a now established feminist tradition of academic writing on popular culture, and some critical reflection on this phenomenon forms part of the project: to what extent, for example, can the term 'post-feminist' be used to describe changes in the texts and audiences of contemporary popular culture? What is the nature of the relationships between researcher and researched, between text and audience, or text and researcher in this and similar projects? First, however, I will explore the place and significance of *Morse* in contemporary British culture: how mainstream is *Morse*?

The escape from enterprise: Englishness and cultural value

Audience ratings are not enough to give cultural status to a television programme, as the fate of any number of soap operas will attest. *Morse* has succeeded both in terms of audience size and as a cultural icon which can be invoked to illustrate and epitomize the term 'quality television'. Before considering any subcultural or subversive readings of *Morse*, it is important to investigate its place in the mainstream, its relation to the dominant culture of the period and the possible reasons for its adoption as icon of quality.

The discourse of quality, despite its literary background, has always been prevalent in discussion of television, which as a medium still struggles for respectability. It could indeed be argued that the definition of certain programmes as quality productions has played a vital role in increasing the cultural status of television, and in countering arguments about its nefarious influence. The recent revival of this debate hardly seems surprising given the new Conservatives' self-appointed role as guardians of British traditions and morality, and Charlotte Brunsdon has described the impact of the White Paper of 1988 on definitions of quality television

(Brunsdon, 1990). According to Brunsdon, the quality discourse, for example in newspaper previews, can comprise traditional aesthetic criteria, professional codes, realist paradigms, entertainment and leisure codes and moral paradigms, though in the White Paper, significantly, mainly moral and realist criteria are used. In her work on the American organization 'Viewers for quality television', Sue Brower has similarly identified a combination of aesthetic concerns and moral values in the organization's definitions of quality; she describes the moral values as '"enlightened", middle-class, liberal, feminist', and argues that the members of the organization use quality as a mask for fan behaviour, and as a way of acquiring status by association (Brower, 1992: 172).

In Britain, both the aesthetic and moral aspects of the discourse are given a particular inflection by the association of quality with Englishness, which furthermore is diametrically opposed to all things American. In the context of crime fiction, this differentiation seems to hinge on factors such as the absence of violent struggles or car chases, a detective who uses his or her intellect rather than physical strength in the fight against crime, and a rural or small-town rather than big-city setting. Even before the first broadcast in January 1987 *Morse* was described in a *Sight and Sound* preview as part of a crusade to reclaim a quintessentially English tradition:

> With this crew, one feels that the English detective story is safe on its home ground with no hankering to convert the middle-aged, edgy maverick of the Thames Valley force into something more chic and Californian.
>
> (Kockenlocker, 1986: 240)

In her use of the term 'Brideshead/Jewel' to define a particular type of quality TV, characterized by its 'heritage export value', Charlotte Brunsdon describes this association of nostalgic nationalism with cultural quality (Brunsdon, 1990: 86). *Morse* shares with the two programmes cited by Brunsdon an iconography of Englishness which became a commonplace of film and television culture in the 1980s, and which can be seen in part as a response to the pressures on British broadcasters to produce exportable television. This visual expression of Englishness requires village greens and gardens, medieval lanes and churches, and wood-panelled interiors where log fires burn even in high summer. In *Morse* none of this is denied us; the tragedy and violence of English middle-class life are revealed and deplored by Morse, and yet the secure routines of tea and dinner, the aesthetic pleasures of a country residence, remain undisturbed. The reviewers frequently seem to have absorbed this aspect of the series so completely that its pleasures are described using the same cosy and domestic imagery of Englishness which the programmes themselves abound in:

FEMINIST REVIEW NO 51, AUTUMN 1995

The plots have a nice comfortable ring to them like Agatha Christie stories re-
written by Iris Murdoch. They remind one of sensible shoes and unchilled
sherry, toasted crumpets and the triumph of good over evil.

(Naughton, 1987: 36)

In his discussion of Merchant/Ivory films, Cairns Craig has linked such
images of Englishness to a national crisis of identity and to the materialism
of the Thatcher years; he reads them both as a search for stability in a
period of radical and destructive change, and as 'conspicuous consumption' colluding with Thatcherite values (Craig, 1991: 10). The narrative
structure of *Morse* certainly seems typical of the crime genre in its playing
out and eventual containment of political and psychic anxieties (Neale,
1980). However, Craig's reading of the Thatcherite values implicit in
Merchant/Ivory should not be grafted on to *Morse*. While there is no
denying the nostalgic nationalism identified by Brunsdon, the very size of
the *Morse* audience suggests an appeal to a wider political and social
spectrum, and the feminine and domestic tone of the programmes can be
seen as out of tune with the more bellicose utterances of Thatcherism.

In general, characters who seem to represent the 'enterprise' culture of the
1980s receive short shrift from Morse and from the plots in which they are
enmeshed. The yuppie Maguire in *Last Seen Wearing* (Zenith, 1988) may
not be implicated in any crime but he is guilty of working as a 'negotiator'
for a Docklands luxury development, and of owning a flat whose black,
white and chrome décor and car-shaped telephone are sufficient grounds
for arrest as far as Morse is concerned. Almost inevitably a house with a
swimming pool indicates foul play, or at the very least, an unhappy
marriage. The conditions of production of *Inspector Morse* seem ironically
typical of a 1980s scenario; it is made by Zenith, a company originally
owned by Central, who initiated the project, and subsequently taken over
by Carlton Communications and Paramount (Sanderson, 1991: 26).
In series six, the credits announced that *Morse* was now 'in association'
with Beamish Stout, thus making an uncomfortable link between the
textual resistance to enterprise, and the reality of the text as commercial
product. If *Morse* has succeeded commercially without completely
espousing the political ethos of its time, it seems relevant to ask whether
the depiction of the private sphere maintains a similarly delicate balance
between conservative and radical elements. Before turning to the gender
politics of the texts I will attempt to place the discussion in the context of
other feminist writing on popular culture.

Feminist readings of popular culture

If generally the term 'postfeminism' implies that gender equality has been
achieved, or was a misguided aim in the first place, in the field of cultural

studies it can be used positively to denote a more sophisticated and multifaceted women's movement, or more often negatively, to describe a recent tendency in the media to put 'liberated' women firmly in their place. Susan Faludi, for instance, has argued that popular culture in the 1980s is characterized by violent reactions against the women's movement. She surveys the press, popular film and television, as well as the fashion and beauty industries in both America and Britain in order to conclude that the positive representations of women of the 1970s have been followed by a cultural backlash, epitomized by the film *Fatal Attraction*, and by 1980s neologisms such as 'cocooning', 'nesting' or 'the mummy track' (Faludi, 1992). Meanwhile, in *The Female Gaze* (Gamman and Marshment, 1988) researchers in Britain give accounts of a struggle to find feminist meanings in popular texts, such as *Cagney and Lacey* or *Desperately Seeking Susan*. Although individual contributions vary, the general trend of this volume is to reject earlier, more pessimistic theories of women's relation to popular culture (Mulvey, 1975), and to claim that feminism has had a significant impact. Even though much of the volume is in fact concerned with political assessment of representations of women, men and sexuality, the articles often conclude that a single politically correct line is to be rejected in favour of resistance through a variety and range of readings. In both cases the choice of texts is crucial, and perhaps dictates the diametrically opposed conclusions reached by the two works: Faludi skims through media and genres in two cultures selecting texts which contain negative representations of single women and lesbians. Texts in *The Female Gaze* are chosen for more detailed study because of their feminist content or potential, thus attention is focused on 'women's' genres, such as blockbuster romance, the film versions of feminist works such as *The Color Purple*, or advertising directed at women.

These two tendencies could be seen as an instance of the conflict between earlier traditions of critique of popular culture by the left, and the more recent desire to celebrate its possibilities for cultural resistance. If the production of meaning is rarely uniform or monolithic, then selections can be made by cultural researchers according to the tendency they wish to support. The only possible conclusion would seem to be that feminism continues to have a profound, if complicated, impact on anglophone popular culture, and that in both the academic and the popular spheres it is out of fashion. The pages of *The Female Gaze* are haunted by the spectre of 'the drab, dungareed dyke' (Gamman and Marshment, 1988: 178), and by tension between the desire both to keep up with these celebratory postfeminist times, and to be critical of negative representations of women.

Although historical genre study would be one way of avoiding the dangers of selectivity, here I have chosen to concentrate on one series, which with audiences of around 15 million is arguably the most resounding television success of the late 1980s and early 1990s. *Morse* does not belong to a 'women's' genre, the main characters are men, and with some exceptions, such as scriptwriter Alma Cullen and producer Deirdre Keir, the production team was predominantly male. If in this sense *Morse* does not belong to the category of text usually subjected to feminist scrutiny, it is all the more significant that the gender politics of the original novels were not thought suitable for television. The analysis of feminist elements within the programmes which follows may therefore provide a case-study of the influence of feminism on an exceptionally popular television series, chosen neither specifically for its appeal to women, nor for its negative representations.

Feminism in the text

From novel to screen

The principal difference between the six *Morse* programmes closely based on the novels by Colin Dexter and the original texts is the relative absence of sexual objectification in the portrayal of the women characters in the TV version. The requirements of quality television in the late 1980s clearly demanded a more subtle approach, and Morse's character has been substantially changed so that the sexually predatory element is replaced by romantic yearning. In *Last Bus to Woodstock* (Zenith, 1988), for example, the television Morse reprimands Lewis for his use of sexist and proprietorial language about his wife and children, while in the novel, Morse leers at the barmaid in the pub where the murder has taken place, and eventually succumbs to the charms of the murderer herself. Whereas in the television version Sylvia Kane's death results from an accidental combination of circumstances, in which the don, Crowther, and his mistress are implicated, in the novel Sylvia's death is caused by a vicious blow from the jealous woman. A similar pattern can be observed in *Last Seen Wearing*; in Dexter's original version the Headmaster is guilty of no major crime, the Deputy Head, Baines, is not even female, let alone lesbian, and the murderer is Valerie, the missing girl herself. In the television version the Headmaster is indirectly responsible for Valerie's disappearance, and directly responsible for the death of Baines, while Valerie is guilty only of adolescent confusion.

The effect of these reversals may be to return women to the traditional status of victim, but Dexter's image of women using their sexuality against men, and showing no qualms in resorting to violence, would be more likely to cause offence or at least the charge of implausibility. The positive representation of a lesbian character in the TV version of *Last Seen Wearing* is only marginally useful to the plot and seems to emphasize the corruption and emptiness of the heterosexual relationships which lead to her death. Although the representation of women generally in the television series is far from radical, characters such as Baines do indicate some acknowledgement that if the TV Morse is a reformed character, the women he encounters need to be more than objects of desire. However, the feminist agenda is perhaps most apparent in those programmes which were written for television. In *Fat Chance* (Zenith, 1991), scripted, significantly, by a woman, Alma Cullen, we see a narrative based on feminist concerns: the ordination of women in the Church of England, and the impact of oppressive stereotypes of female beauty on adolescent girls. Zoë Wanamaker plays a character exemplifying the conventionally irreconcilable – a penchant for Italian designer suits and feminist politics. When Morse receives her seal of approval, having championed the feminist cause throughout, we are inclined to agree with her that he really is 'one of the good guys'.

Single virtue versus married vice

All around Morse, heterosexuality, particularly of the married kind, wreaks havoc. It is unremarkable that *Morse*, along with a great deal of crime fiction, should manifest the deeply rooted cultural association of death and sexuality, but the repeated castigation of the morals of married men lends added significance to the emotional purity of Morse's single life, or even, though to a lesser extent, to Lewis's cosily asexual conjugal bliss. With Lewis as the notable exception, married men deceive their bored and frustrated wives and exploit the vulnerability of the single women they seduce, sometimes, as in *The Dead of Jericho* (Zenith, 1987), leading them to degradation, despair and death. Morse oscillates between the generic requirement of celibacy (see Wilson, 1988), and the strong romantic tendencies of the character and the plots. His singleness is obsessively referred to in lines such as: 'Chastity and continence, when did I ever have anything else?' from *Service of All the Dead* (Zenith, 1987), and the contrast between Morse and the happily married Lewis is fundamental to the structure of the programmes. Murderers, potential victims and the relatives of victims all take the opportunity, on encountering Morse, to enquire after his marital status, and to contrast his singleness with their own entanglements. In general, the family is a vipers' nest, and symbols of affluence almost always guarantee the deadliness of its occupants.

It is presumably safe to assume, none the less, that the writers and producers of the television series are not 'engagés' in the fight against Thatcherite family values, and that these negative images of married and family life have come to perform some crucial function in the development of the character and charisma of Morse. If Morse is surrounded by

Photograph by Central ITV shows John Thaw as Chief Inspector Morse and Kevin Whately as Sergeant Lewis. Photograph © Central ITV.

examples of male perfidy, they serve to highlight the idealized masculinity which he represents. Lewis also has his part to play in the depiction of an acceptable masculinity, but while his ability to cope with the modern demands of companionate marriage, shared childcare and DIY are admirable, unlike our hero he cannot sustain the emotional limelight. In the first instance Morse is deeply moral; he plays the traditional role of the detective as representative and upholder of the Law and is always on the right side in the universal battle between good and evil, which the crimes of passion he investigates often seem to invoke. Morse expresses righteous anger on the victims' behalf, and the programmes frequently end with a soliloquy on the wicked ways of men, which may include a quotation from a work of literature, and is often set against shots of Oxford's awe-inspiring architectural beauty. Morse can never resist the opportunity to point out who is the real villain of the piece, and as, for example, in *Deadly Slumber* (Zenith, 1993), is particularly enraged by the prioritization of money-making over human life. In this sense Morse is out of tune with the times, simultaneously liberal rebel and avenging patriarch, but above all passionate in his pursuit of justice.

A new/old masculinity

The difference between Morse and ordinary men does not, however, lie solely in his stern righteousness, and there are indeed times when his involvement with a guilty party clouds his judgement. Perhaps it is the combination of the traditionally paternal qualities described above with an ability to nurture which makes Morse blessed among men. Morse willingly provides a shoulder to cry on and is a sensitive and perceptive listener. At times the tasks of nurturing others and punishing crime are in conflict, as in *Deadly Slumber*, where Morse's sensitivity to the tragedy of Michael Steppings' daughter makes him rather too willing to cross Steppings off the list of suspects. If this ability to give emotionally renders Morse a less effective policeman, it may do a lot for the audience ratings. In her analysis of the appeal of romantic fiction, based on Freud, Amal Treacher has argued that the romantic hero nurtures as well as dominates the heroine, and that it is in this representation of a hero who is both ideal mother and ideal father that the emotional satisfactions of such works lie for their largely female readership (Treacher, 1988). Something of this kind may be in play here; without doubt parenting is a theme in *Morse*, and it is a theme which was not present in the original novels. If the 1980s 'new man' of the advertisements has failed as an icon of anything more than a hollow self-sufficiency, perhaps Morse's attempts to father and mother are a more resonant fantasy for male and female viewers.

But what of Morse's own needs? We return again to romance, and to the appeal of Morse's own vulnerability. Morse, like the operas he immerses himself in, is a vehicle for the expression of grand emotion. Unlike other male detectives, or for that matter the Morse of the Dexter novels, emotion rather than intellect is his true medium. Although the Inspector goes through the motions of thinking, it is increasingly Lewis who has the brainwaves, while Morse relies on that most feminine of skills, intuition. In this sense Morse, despite his traditional appearance, is breaking through boundaries, both of gender and genre. In *Dead on Time* (Zenith, 1992), Morse's new/old masculinity may have strayed even beyond its own parameters; the sight of Morse sobbing over the corpse of his former fiancée and the provision of an 'explanation' for his moodiness were dangerous developments. But *Dead on Time* allowed Lewis to make his contribution to the image of caring manhood, and it seemed fortunate that a sensitive soul such as Morse should have Lewis to watch over him. While the programmes continually depict the secure and civilized pleasures of Morse's home-life – the music, good wine and tranquil lounging on the sofa – an encounter with an attractive woman 'd'un certain âge' inevitably rekindles a poignant and disorientating longing for intimacy. Morse does all those old-fashioned things which are eschewed by the new man or irrelevant in the more prosaic world of Lewis; he sends flowers, asks women out and pays touching if clumsy compliments. The fact that none of this ever leads to anything remotely resembling a relationship is a further

FEMINIST REVIEW NO 51, AUTUMN 1995

enhancement of his charms. Morse remains the ideal lover, always more involved than the woman in question, and not afraid to admit it. Detection and romance thus combine admirably, since the requirement for celibacy in the former creates an enticing lack, the ultimate romance narrative where the threat of satisfaction, and hence of the loss of desire is removed (see Neale, 1980).

Introducing the audience

Quality television and fan culture

The popularity of *Morse*, and the amount of media attention which the audience itself has received, indicate that textual analysis in isolation would be to reduce to text alone a cultural phenomenon which also encompasses secondary literature, consumer goods such as audio and video tapes, experiences such as '*Morse* tours' and the fan culture generated by, and generating, such ephemera. The *Morse* audience is variously represented in the reviews as object of statistical analysis or as subject, with the reviewer identifying as a fan and meditating on the pleasures of the programmes. In the first case the audience tends to be described as middle class and middle aged, or more technically as 'ABC1 adults aged 35+' (MacArthur, 1990: 25). In the second, humour is a protection from the excesses of mindless fandom:

> Morse is back! There was, I think, a fresh spring in my step. I spent the day in anxious reverie. What would it be like? After months of youthful repeats, would the new series simply confirm that nothing stands the test of time? Or could the old red Jaguar still do two hours in what always seemed a mere 40 minutes?

> (Newnham, 1992: 29)

If the statistics produce an image too general to be of interest outside the advertising world, the self-reflective irony of the article quoted above suggests that being a fan of a quality series is not without its complexities. Jensen has argued that fandom is often represented as an irrational and excessive cult of a low-status cultural form (Jensen, 1992). It is therefore not surprising that despite the evidence of 'fan' behaviour, the popularity of *Morse* is rarely discussed in such terms. In contrast to the low status of television as a medium, *Morse* aspires to cultural respectability, and to be a devotee of the series may therefore have altogether different connotations from those usually associated with TV fandom. The audience research described in the final part of this piece was particularly concerned to investigate how these contradictions might be experienced and expressed by fans of the series.

Feminism and audience study

Perhaps the danger of selecting texts and reading them according to a pre-set agenda can be avoided, at least to some extent, by combining textual analysis with audience study. It would seem likely that here, if anywhere, the frequently invoked polysemy might be found. If feminism has a role, then its presence will be felt not only in texts, but also in the talk about texts which it could be argued is the place where popular culture 'happens'. One aim of this research was to explore how feminism might inform such talk, and how feminist elements in the text are taken up in particular social contexts, in this case discussion groups and telephone interviews. Although I did not attempt to recruit feminist fans specifically, gender politics emerged as the main preoccupation in one of the discussion groups, and some telephone interviews. As a result I was able to explore questions about the nature of a particular subculture which seemed to be expressing itself in the discussion of *Morse*, the kinds of subject positions which were adopted within it, the reading strategies and discourses which it generated. I was also concerned with the paradox of a subcultural adoption of a highly conventional mainstream text. Inevitably, if I was exploring how talk about television in the 1990s might be influenced by feminism, I was doing so in the era of 'post-feminism', and although impossible to prove, it seemed likely that such talk would differ significantly from similar conversations in the early years of the women's movement. Finally, my research is small-scale and can only claim to have investigated a few instances of feminist subculture, or *Morse* fan culture; its limitations and the peculiarities of the social events I am analysing are discussed in detail below.

The research process

If my own reading had identified the critique of heterosexuality and the search for an acceptable masculinity as instances of textual engagement with feminist issues, it remained to be seen whether this would be recognized by other regular viewers, and how they might negotiate the polarities quality/fandom or feminism/traditionalism. In audience work by feminist researchers, a cultural gulf may develop between the researcher and the researched, whose tastes are secretly disapproved of. The researcher may express ambivalence resulting from the conflict between identification with a women's genre such as romantic fiction and with the women who are the subjects of the research, and feminist political correctness. These issues have been raised by Janice Radway in a critique of her earlier work on readers of romantic fiction, in which she describes how despite intending to affirm the romance readers' culture, she in the end distanced herself as 'knowing analyst' from them (Radway, 1994: 214).

Although my desire to write about *Morse* was dictated initially more by my own involvement with the series than by academic considerations, I have inevitably acquired a certain status as researcher and cannot claim to be free of these contradictions. Throughout the discussion, I have therefore attempted to reflect on, and wherever possible to clarify, my own role and position.

An answer to the question of how to contact *Morse* fans was provided by the NFT's decision to screen a John Thaw season in September 1991, including one episode of *Morse*. I distributed questionnaires at the screening (*The Dead of Jericho*) which asked people who might be willing to participate in a discussion group or telephone interview to give their name, address, occupation, age group, and reason for attending the screening. Out of an audience of about 100, 30 completed questionnaires were collected. The sample was white, predominantly though not exclusively middle class, and young (75 per cent under 35). Some months later, in April 1992, while a new series of *Morse* was being screened on ITV, this sample of 30 were contacted again, and asked whether they would be willing to participate in a telephone interview. Thirteen responded positively and nine interviews ranging from 10 to 40 minutes in length were carried out. These were followed by two discussion evenings at the then Polytechnic of North London.

Here I will concentrate on the second of the two groups, where the content of the discussion developed in such a way as to be highly relevant to the theme of this article. By this stage it seemed likely that the participants, who by now had responded to two further approaches, were keen *Morse* fans, rather than just cinema-goers who happened to be at the NFT that evening. None the less, the culture of both discussion groups was very clearly white and metropolitan, and a geographical location outside London or a greater ethnic diversity may well have produced very different results. The composition of the group was as follows:

Lisa: mid-twenties, postgraduate psychology student
Sarah: late twenties, postgraduate psychology student
Sue: late thirties, civil servant
Joan: late fifties, unemployed
Jim: early thirties, civil servant

An interested colleague, Karen, attended the session as an observer; Karen and I were both lecturers at the then Polytechnic of North London, in our late thirties, and Karen is German. Food and wine were provided, and four extracts from *Inspector Morse* (chosen for their relevance to the issues of gender representation discussed on pp. 7–10) were screened, with time for discussion after each one. The extracts were:

1 The last five minutes of *The Dead of Jericho* (first broadcast on 6 January 1987).

2 Morse and Lewis interviewing the Headmaster and his family in *Last Seen Wearing* (first broadcast on 8 March 1988).

3 From the same programme, Morse interviewing the Deputy Head-mistress, Miss Baines, in her house late at night, immediately prior to her death during a row with the Head, who pushes her downstairs.

4 The scene from *Dead on Time* (first broadcast on 26 April 1992), when Morse entertains Susan, his former fiancée.

Morse as 'lived experience'

The social context

Adopting the categories proposed by Fairclough (1989), and already applied to the analysis of children's talk about television by Buckingham (1993), I have analysed the discussions in terms of *relations* between group members and *subject positions* adopted, as well as content. This approach aims to avoid the danger of assuming that people say what they mean in any simple sense, and to counteract the tendency of much previous work in this area to divorce meaning from the social context in which it is produced. In practice it was difficult to separate subject positions from relations, since the adoption of the former is a crucial part of the latter. In the section below, therefore, a consideration of the groups' relationships with each other leads into a discussion of subject positions adopted by group members, and the dividing line is inevitably blurred.

Despite the food and wine provided, the setting for the discussions was unmistakably educational, and it is possible to identify a tension between the 'party' connotations of the plentiful supplies of food and wine and the far from luxurious classroom setting. The slightly guilty tones, or suggestions that I should switch off the tape-recorder when someone asked for more wine suggest that the event was perceived more as a class than a party, though particularly in this case, where at least half the group was likely to be very at home in an educational context, the atmosphere became increasingly relaxed as the evening progressed, and there were many occasions for laughter. A detailed analysis of my interventions shows that I was mainly in 'teacher' mode. Seventy per cent of my interventions had functions such as:

– introducing new subjects/asking questions
– addressing a named person
– following up a point
– summarizing or reflecting back

– giving information about the programmes

– structuring/organizing the event

The fact that for 30 per cent of the time I participated as a fan, recounting the plot, telling jokes or occasionally commenting on programmes, none the less indicates that I was split between my conscious intention to behave as a neutral facilitator of the discussion, and the desire to participate in the group, and switch to 'fellow fan' mode. The implications of this for the discussion are analysed more fully below. Here, it is sufficient to note that the combination of being one of the group some of the time and in the powerful position of teacher/researcher the rest means that the cultural agenda which I set is likely to play a significant role in the development of the discussion.

The group dynamics in this discussion seem particularly influenced by gender difference. The fact of being the only man in the group seems to have elicited certain types of response from Jim, who seems concerned to make an impression on the others and even to obtain a dominant position. This behaviour was met with opposition, at times verging on hostility, both from the group members and from myself. I certainly saw keeping Jim under control and sabotaging his attempts at dominance as an important part of my role as discussion facilitator. After the discussion Karen commented that it had been a women-dominated group, and I felt rather guilty about treating Jim unfairly. When the tape was played to a (mixed) group of fellow researchers they commented that Jim had had a hard time, and it was indeed the case that I silenced him on several occasions during this short extract. It is therefore interesting that counting the number of lines spoken by each person reveals that Jim spoke more than anyone other than Sarah, and that he introduced more new subjects than anyone other than myself. The fact that the representation of women in *Inspector Morse* became a major theme in this group, whereas this was not the case in the other discussion group, has to be seen in the context of this gender-based power struggle. There is no doubt that this theme was a common area of interest uniting Sarah, Lisa, Sue and myself, but the fact that it was taken up with such energy, and returned to so repeatedly, must to some extent be the result of these rather particular group dynamics.

The discussion was analysed both by means of a simple line count and a 'map' of the introduction of new topics. This information revealed that in this group, the participant most involved in the representation of women theme, Sarah, is also the dominant member of the group. She introduces relatively few new topics, but she speaks most, is most responsible for the fact that certain areas are developed, and is most frequently the first to respond to questions which I asked. The fact that she was sitting opposite me and that empathy was expressed through eye contact and laughing loudly at each others' jokes meant that Sarah assumed a 'star pupil' role, and that to some extent a new and particularly powerful friendship pair was formed within the group. Given that Sarah and Lisa, and Joan and Sue had come as pairs of friends, it would be possible to comment that the all-female couple was a subtext for the group, and that this provides an interesting context for the discussion of the images of heterosexual couples presented in the *Morse* extracts. The agenda set by these friendship pairs, and by my role, was undoubtedly that of educated, white, middle-class feminism. Sarah, Lisa, Sue, Karen and I were all in our twenties or thirties, and our class position was broadly similar, even if the trajectory we had followed to arrive at it may well have been different, and was not the subject of this research. The common culture which operated in this subgroup is perhaps most evident in the intertextual references, particularly to soap opera, where in the form of jokes there was a certain amount of feminist 'reclaiming' of apparently conventional texts such as *The Archers* (BBC Radio, 1951–). The subject position which I and these group members adopted seemed to be that of critical reader, whose status in feminist alternative culture gives her permission to enjoy 'ideologically unsound' popular texts.

Jim was excluded from this position by gender, and perhaps by educational background, and seemed more concerned to establish himself as critical reader in terms of knowledge of the programmes and the production process, and ability to evaluate quality. Joan's position was more complex, in that she participated very little in the discussion and in that sense could be seen as far more excluded than Jim. This may be attributable to her age (over 55) and employment status, which differentiated her from the other women present. Perhaps because of these factors my attempts to bring her into the discussion were unsuccessful. Although Joan spoke very little, she introduced one entirely new area to the discussion (the theme of 'pastness' in *Morse*), and at times adopted an oppositional position in relation to Jim:

> **Jim:** But the story is about a male detective and his male sidekick
>
> **Sue:** Yeah but I bet the audience is mostly women
>
> **Jim:** Well I mean OK you know I don't go for middle-aged grey-haired men er I mean I'm outnumbered here
>
> **Joan:** I might
>
> (General laughter).

As this extract shows, Joan is very much part of the oppositional 'women's culture' of the group, and here she introduces the topic of 'fancying' Morse which is developed later by other group members. She is also involved in

FEMINIST REVIEW NO 51, AUTUMN 1995

subverting Jim's overtly masculine point of view. At the same time she is perhaps differentiating herself from the younger women. Despite this, and the fact that the ages in this group range from early twenties to late fifties, some kind of a consensus emerged from the discussion of the representation of youth culture in *Cherubim and Seraphim* (Zenith, 1992); Sue was instrumental in this in referring to herself as 'an old fart' and thus making the only overt statement about age. The subject position adopted by Sue was clearly approved of by the women in the group, who laughed loudly at this point, and despite the presence of two very young women, being older and listening to Radio 4 rather than Acidhouse seemed to form part of the feminist cultural identity being constructed in the discussion. This older identity may result from the fact that many 'second-wave' feminists are now in their late thirties or forties, and this may therefore be a more culturally established position than 'young feminist'. The feminist construction of younger women as 'other' exemplified in the last lines of Shelagh Young's piece in *The Female Gaze*, may contribute to this:

> We could start by listening to the views of those wayward daughters who seem to be so actively resisting, rather than conforming to, any simple feminist model of the New Woman. After all, there must be that little bit of a feminist subject lurking in there somewhere, mustn't there? And if there is, I suspect she's looking back at me.
>
> (Young, 1988: 188)

In this case the younger women manifested a desire to contribute to a group identity based on gender and feminist politics, rather than gazing critically on the latter. The youth theme also led to a heated discussion of class, as Jim's mis-recognition of the youth subculture provoked an indignant response:

> **Jim:** I think you can tell I'm middle class. I've never had any experience of that but from what I know and from what you read in the papers and what you hear I think all that sort of underclass culture I think it was toned down
> **Lisa:** I don't think it was underclass culture
> **Lyn:** They were middle class
> (All talk at once)
> **Lisa:** It was a youth culture
> **Several voices:** Yes.

In educational terms, it may well be that Jim is less middle class than most of the women present, and his claim may be an expression of resulting feelings of insecurity. The almost angry response of the other group members perhaps also denotes an anxiety in this area. Mis-recognition of a middle-class person as working class may be particularly threatening to an insecure subject position resulting either from a move from working class to middle class, or from a middle-class person's political empathy with less privileged groups. In general the subject position in relation to class adopted by Sarah, Lisa and Sue is certainly a long way from Jim's statement, and they refer repeatedly to the rich people on *Morse*, who are outside their normal experience. Another heated argument erupts when Lisa accuses the programme-makers of ignoring working-class Oxford, and Jim explains their financial motivations for this to her:

> **Jim:** But what the Oxford City Council or whoever it is wants to portray, they want to portray sort of dreaming spires and punting down the river, things like that, you know to get the tourists in . . . (Passage omitted)
> **Lisa:** (angrily) But I expect it's not the people who need the money that are getting it.

In this instance, and in the repeated distancing from wealthy characters, an oppositional position in relation to 'middle-classness' is being adopted, as part of the alternative feminist culture which pervaded the discussion. It is therefore not surprising that Jim's more aspirational statement was met with disapproval.

Critical reading and emotional involvement

The discussion of *Morse* is perhaps unlike talk about other television programmes less obviously stamped with the quality label; because the programmes themselves, and all the literature surrounding them, are concerned to differentiate *Morse* from less polished products, it may be the case that to be a *Morse* fan is in some sense to associate oneself with this cultural superiority, negotiating fandom in the same way as members of 'Viewers for quality television' in Sue Brower's account (see p. 3 above). Given the oppositional position in relation to 'middle-classness' discussed above, the negotiation of this area in this group was likely to be a complex matter. Although quality was a less dominant theme than gender representation, it was referred to in the discussion, which made conventional associations of quality with high production values, realism, the intellectual challenge of the plots, and the character of Morse himself:

> **Sue:** It's supposed to be, you know this is an intellectual
> **Sarah:** It's extremely, he's not listening to 'Right Said Fred' and drinking brown ale here
> **Lisa:** He can't possibly understand the wide real world [ ]
> **Jim:** Good stuff that. I don't see why he shouldn't do that. I'm not a particular fan of classical music but a lot of [what] Morse listens to, is a darned sight better than what you get on television nowadays
> **Sarah:** He is a sort of cultured man, he doesn't spend his evening with his feet up watching *EastEnders*. He is listening to that particularly good recording of Verdi with a nice bottle of wine or something. The way whenever he goes to a

FEMINIST REVIEW NO 51, AUTUMN 1995

pub he doesn't just go to a pub he goes in one that's got good draught ale. It's always very quality.

As this extract shows, there are at least two kinds of relation to the concept of quality in this discussion: while Jim is anxious to claim the ability to differentiate Morse from lower quality texts, in this case popular as opposed to classical music, Sarah and Sue are taking up a position of critical distance, able to appreciate the connotations of Morse's 'quality' tastes, without necessarily associating themselves with them. For them what is at stake is the demonstration of the ability to read the signs, rather than the capacity to be impressed by them. Jim, on the other hand is anxious to affirm his middle-class status, by claiming the ability to appreciate classical music, which according to Pierre Bourdieu is a particularly significant cultural marker:

> For a bourgeois world which conceives its relation to the populace in terms of the relationship of the soul to the body, 'insensitivity to music' doubtless represents a particularly unavowable form of materialist coarseness.
>
> (Bourdieu, 1979: 19)

Whereas Jim attempts to align himself with Morse's musical superiority, the other members of the group are reading off precisely the meaning defined by Bourdieu, and thus demonstrating their ability to interpret the significant elements of the Morse character, and hence to be aware of its constructed nature. Jim's attempts to acquire 'cultural capital' in this context, where he does not belong to the critical subculture being developed, consist partly, as here, in recognizing the quality aspects of the programmes, and partly in explaining *how* and *why* things are done. Ellen Seiter has described how in an interview with two men about soap opera, one of the men seemed most concerned to impress the 'high status' academics doing the interview by showing off his factual knowledge. Seiter uses Bourdieu to explain why such attempts are doomed to failure, and to position herself and her colleague as 'legitimate autodidacts' who have a stake in the maintenance of this particular cultural and social divide (Seiter, 1990: 65–6). Seiter's discussion seems particularly pertinent to the analysis of Jim's position in this group, where his knowledge is constantly rejected as illegitimate, or inappropriate to the academic setting and cultural agenda set by the other group members and myself. Jim's concern is to demonstrate that he knows how television programmes are put together, and while he expresses cynicism about the programme-makers' intentions the tone of his discussion is one of acceptance, that this is how things of necessity have to be. In this again, he is at odds with the rest of the group, who are questioning precisely this inevitability:

Jim: You've got to remember that it's rich people that make sort of interesting characters. I mean sort of people that do boring mundane jobs and sort of come home in the evening and watch telly and go to bed, I mean where's the interest in that?

Sue: What about *Coronation Street*?

(Laughter).

Although the high production standards of *Morse* are referred to in this group, criticism is more prevalent than praise. This of course does not mean that the group members are indifferent to this aspect of the programmes, merely that in this context they feel that it is more appropriate to be critical:

Lisa: It's still compelling viewing it really is. It's compelling sort of viewing. I would do anything not to miss, I mean most things I don't bother videoing it if I'm going to be out, but Morse definitely you know. I've even learnt how to set the video to do it. But yes OK you can be critical, but then I think you're partly asking us to be critical.

This sense of being asked to be critical may be a response to the educational setting, and it is significant that those most used to operating in this context felt this.

The association of quality with Englishness discussed on pp. 2–5 above was introduced here by the oldest participant, Joan, indicating perhaps that her silence may be the result of a different range of interests from the rest of the group; at this point there is a departure from the predominant feminist critique, and Sarah, who is extremely active in the rest of the discussion, is significantly silent:

Joan: *Morse* to me never seems to be current. It seems to be in the past. I don't know how far back in the past, not that far back [ ]

Lisa: It's the whole thing about Oxford and the setting as well isn't it?

Joan: Yes

Lisa: I mean it's a very sort of antiquated setting in a way and when you hear the word sort of Oxford you assume that you're talking about you know the university and [the sort of buildings

Jim: [Too much dreaming spires and students on pushbikes.

Lisa seems able to recognize and identify with what Joan is saying and she later returns to this theme in one of the rare moments where an emotional, as opposed to intellectual pleasure is discussed:

Lisa: The trouble with all these little digressions into Australia and Italy and subcultures or whatever, I don't know I actually like the old formula and the sort of almost the predictability of the Oxford and the car and you know all these little things.

The sense of reassurance and security described here is reminiscent of the reviews, and may be an expression of the process of containment of anxiety by a television narrative (see pp. 3–4 above). The satisfactions afforded by familiarity are, however, more frequently disavowed, displaced by critique of the repetitiveness of the plots or the stereotyping of the characters, just as in general critical distance rather than emotional involvement is the predominant mode of talking about the programmes in this discussion.

Feminism and popular romance

It is in the area of romance that the tension between the expression of pleasure and the establishment of status as critical reader is most marked. The romance plot seems to be the aspect of the programmes which this group finds most fascinating, since it is introduced early in the discussion of each extract, and occupies more time than any other single topic. To some extent the choice of extracts set this particular agenda. However, in the other discussion group the topic is not developed to the same extent. On the contrary, in several of the telephone interviews, which were of course independent of this screening, romance again emerged as a preoccupation. Although I chose the extracts because of their relevance to my own reading of the negative representation of the family and the heterosexual couple (see p. 7 above), this may not be obvious to spectators who are not specifically trained to be aware of issues of representation, as the first discussion group would seem to attest. Even in this group, where the representation issue was addressed, the theme which I saw as the common thread linking the extracts did not emerge as significant, and it was the related but distinct question of the representation of women which became an almost obsessive concern. Here a great deal of critical energy was generated, as Sarah, Sue and Lisa poured scorn on the 'pathetic' women characters:

> Lisa: They're very peripheral to the stories I think if they're not actually involved with Morse directly
> Jim: But the story is about a male detective and his male sidekick
> Sue: Yeah but I would think its audience is mostly women.

This extract amply illustrates how critique is functioning as a way of acquiring and expressing solidarity as women, culminating in the view that 'we are the audience'. It is also interesting that the presence of the romance plot in the programmes and this group's preoccupation with it leads to a reversal of the conventional association of crime fiction with masculinity. It would, however, be wrong to conflate criticism of this kind with the absence of emotion, for while distance from the text is certainly expressed, usually in the form of irony, emotions such as anger, or indignation as here, do surface, indicating a passionate engagement with the programmes. The more positive feelings usually associated with romance do none the less seem incompatible with the feminist persona who haunts this discussion. The talk about one of the most romantic episodes, *Dead on Time*, is dominated by criticism of the episode's implausibility, the cliché of the romantic dinner à deux, Morse's besottedness and the heroine's coy femininity, but immediately after the screening, before the critical mood gains momentum, Lisa expresses her feelings about the extract:

> **Lisa:** [ ] It was so sort of touching, wasn't it, Lewis sort of protecting him from the knowledge right the way through to the end and he never told him right at the end and considering the hard time Morse always gives Lewis and you know the barking at him in the office and for getting things wrong and when he has actually got something right he only, because it's too painful for Morse he doesn't tell him. I thought that was such a sweet thing for Lewis to do.

It is significant that this rare instance of emotional response to the text is focused on the Morse/Lewis relationship rather than on the romance plot itself. None the less, some of the identifications and readings proposed as possible sources of pleasure (see pages 9–10), do seem to operate in some form here. Early in the discussion awareness of the narrative necessity of Morse's unsuccessful romantic life was evident:

> **Jim:** I mean if he hadn't stuck his oar in or whatever she'd still be alive and perhaps Morse would be enjoying a successful love life
> **Sue:** Can't have that
> (Loud laughter).

This was repeated later when Jim's suggestion – 'The Sergeant Lewis Show' – was greeted with horror, on the grounds that since Lewis is happily married, there could be 'no development'. The opportunities for identification provided by the gap in the text left by Morse's inconclusive affairs could not be embraced wholeheartedly in this context, but the use of irony did permit the expression of the fantasy. In this way it was possible simultaneously to remain outside the text, and to enter into it, by filling the gap in the narrative:

> **Sarah:** You imagine you know that he would say 'take off your glasses, why Miss Smith you're beautiful'
> (Loud laughter)
> **Sarah:** He noticed me *yes*. I think that's the secret of it, he's so involved in his work, that if he does notice someone it's something special
> (More laughter).

The energy of the female laughter here indicates partly that Sarah has achieved exactly the right balance – moderating the image of starry-eyed fan by her subtle and ironic intertextual reference, and partly it may be

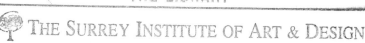

FEMINIST REVIEW NO 51, AUTUMN 1995

releasing any anxiety generated by Sarah's crossing of the diegetic boundary. Immediately before this section, the fantasy of being the woman with whom Morse would at last be happy was linked to the combination of vulnerability and ability to nurture also discussed in pages 9–10 above:

Jim: You know do the women here [.] you know do you like John Thaw?
Sue:] Oh yes
Lisa:] He's terribly attractive
Sue: Yeah you know because the idea is that you're the person who understands him and he's had a really shitty life
Sarah: He's a sad man, who'd love you.

Ann Rosalind Jones has analysed the impact of feminism on contemporary romantic fiction in terms of a transformed power relationship between hero and heroine, based on textual evidence of his vulnerability (Jones, 1986). Here Morse's vulnerability may be attractive to these feminist critical readers in a similar way, seeming to offer a reversal of the pattern common both in fiction and in women's experience of heterosexuality, where male emotional needs are often masked by projection on to the woman. Wendy Hollway has analysed how the positioning of the woman as the subject of what she describes as the 'have/hold discourse' results in emotional inequality, with the woman always needier than her male partner (Hollway, 1992). This syndrome was already transparent to Simone de Beauvoir in the 1940s; in *Le Deuxième Sexe* she provides a detailed analysis of the process whereby women's prioritization of relationships leads them to a dependent role where they are forever trying to ensnare the man into spending more of his precious time with them, while he is anxious to escape in order to realize his many projects in life (de Beauvoir, 1949). With Morse masculinity has come full circle, and the closing images of *Promised Land* (Zenith, 1991) demonstrate the penalties of the avoidance of intimacy: Morse stands alone and desolate on the steps of the Sydney opera house, while Lewis goes off to fill in time before the impending arrival of Mrs Lewis. Like de Beauvoir the women in this group feel that the problem of femininity or at least of these representations of it is the lack of projects, of something to do in life:

Sarah: You know if somewhere in Oxford it was not just entirely populated with attractive 45-year-old women
Sue: Blonde (laughter)
Sarah: (laughs) All blonde
Jim: Yeah but]
Lisa:] They're incompetent. I mean there are competent women around aren't there]

| Sarah: |] Yes and they're always] |
| Sue: |] Who do jobs rather than hanging around waiting to be |

screwed by Morse.

However, unlike de Beauvoir they seem aware of the limitations of traditional masculinity; the appeal of *Morse* is that despite Morse's evident devotion to duty, the programmes present the inadequacies of a work-orientated existence. Morse's neediness, his constant pursuit of 'attractive 45-year-old women' seems here to be providing the beginnings of a feminist fantasy where female power can be combined with romance.

Conclusion

The first part of this article illustrates the complex balancing of conservative and more radical elements in a 'quality' television series of the late 1980s and early 1990s. The programmes oscillate between critique of the status quo and visual affirmation of the securities of English middle-class life, between castigation of heterosexual behaviour and pure romance and, in the case of the hero himself, between the ability to nurture others and his own neediness. The existence of these tensions in the text creates the possibility for a range of readings and identifications, and may be one of the aspects of the series which has ensured its success in winning large audiences. The analysis of the discussion group in the second part of the article indicates how the image of a uniform, mass audience perpetuated by statistical research, masks the range and subtlety of readings and specific fan cultures which a programme such as this may generate. Two aspects of this research, at least, have also been identified in other audience studies (see Buckingham, 1993). Firstly, the readings produced here are specific to this particular social interaction and, in this sense, the social dynamics are at least as significant a factor as the text itself in defining the discourses within which the programme may be discussed. Secondly, participants in this kind of research are understandably anxious to demonstrate that they are not duped by the media. Although this tendency may be heightened in the research situation, it seems likely, given the low status attributed to television as a medium, and to 'fan' behaviour, that presenting oneself as not 'taken in' by the media may be a general feature of talk of this kind.

In this case, the particular versions of this distanced position were 'feminist critical reader' for most of the women present, and 'well-informed cynic about the media' in Jim's case. In the case of the former, the women in the group, including myself, were united by educational level, and by feminist politics, and middle-class, educated feminism became the dominant discourse. As a result of his inability to participate in this discourse, Jim became the least powerful member of the group. While recognizing the small scale of this research, I would guess that the feminist culture expressed in this discussion is not an isolated phenomenon. It seems unlikely that the women in the group could have mobilized discourses such as critique of the representation of women with such alacrity if such discourses were not already well established in some middle-class, educated circles. In this sense, the analysis of feminist influences at work in the text, and of feminism as dominant discourse in this particular discussion suggests that a certain kind of feminism, at least, has a significant, if at times uneasy place in mainstream popular culture in 1990s Britain. The complex position of feminism as both oppositional culture and part of the mainstream is indicated here by the group members' subtle negotiation of such issues as the conflict between feminist critique and romance as a conventionally 'feminine' pleasure. Perhaps most significant are the sense of a feminist identity espousing the 'middle-aged' pleasures of Radio 4 or quality television drama, and the role of irony in this identity, whether directed at the romantic excesses of the text, or at the 'boring old fart' herself.

Notes

I would like to thank Betty and Terry Doonan for their invaluable help in transcribing the tapes.

Lyn Thomas is Senior Lecturer in French at the University of North London. Her research interests are French and British popular culture and contemporary French women's writing.

References

BEAUVOIR, Simone de (1949) *Le Deuxième Sexe* Paris: Editions Gallimard.

BOURDIEU, Pierre (1979) *Distinction: A Social Critique of the Judgement of Taste* translated 1984 by Richard Nice, London: Routledge & Kegan Paul.

BROWER, Sue (1992) 'Fans as tastemakers: viewers for quality television', in Lewis (1992).

BRUNSDON, Charlotte (1990) 'Problems with quality', *Screen* Vol. 31, No. 1: 67–90.

BUCKINGHAM, David (1993) *Children Talking Television* London: The Falmer Press.

CRAIG, Cairns (1991) 'Rooms without a view' *Sight and Sound* Vol. 1, Issue 2, June 1991: 10–13.

CRUZ, Jon and LEWIS, Justin (1994) editors, *Viewing, Reading, Listening: Audiences and Cultural Reception* Boulder and Oxford: Westview Press.

FAIRCLOUGH, Norman (1989) *Language and Power* London: Longman.

FALUDI, Susan (1992) *Backlash: The Undeclared War Against Women* London: Vintage.

GAMMAN, Lorraine and MARSHMENT, Margaret (1988) editors, *The Female Gaze: Women as Viewers of Popular Culture* London: The Women's Press.

HOLLWAY, Wendy (1992) 'Gender difference and the production of subjectivity' in Crowley, Helen and Himmelweit, Susan (1992) editors, *Knowing Women: Feminism and Knowledge* London: Polity Press and The Open University.

JENSEN, Joli (1992) 'Fandom as pathology: the consequences of characterization', in **Lewis** (1992).

JONES, Ann Rosalind (1986) 'Mills and Boon meets feminism', in Radford, Jean (1986) editor, *The Politics of Popular Fiction* London: Routledge & Kegan Paul.

KOCKENLOCKER (1986) 'High Tecs' *Sight and Sound* Vol. 55, No. 4: 240–1.

LEWIS, Lisa (1992) editor, *The Adoring Audience: Fan Culture and Popular Media* London and New York: Routledge.

MACARTHUR, Brian (1990) 'Watching the detectives' *The Guardian* 10 December: 25.

MULVEY, Laura (1975) 'Visual pleasure and narrative cinema' *Screen* Vol. 16, No. 3: 6–18.

NAUGHTON, John (1987) 'Ahead of the pack' *The Listener* Vol. 117, No. 2995, 22 January: 36.

NEALE, Stephen (1980) *Genre* London: British Film Institute.

NEWNHAM, David (1992) 'Goofy over Mickey Morse' *The Guardian* February 27: 29.

POTTER, Jonathan and WETHERELL, Margaret (1987) *Discourse and Social Psychology: Beyond Attitudes and Behaviour* London: Sage Publications (see pp. 188–9 for transcription conventions).

RADWAY, Janice (1994) 'Romance and the work of fantasy: struggles over feminine sexuality and subjectivity at century's end', in **Cruz** and **Lewis** (1994).

SANDERSON, Mark (1991) *The Making of Inspector Morse* London: Macmillan.

SEITER, Ellen (1990) 'Making distinctions in TV audience research: case study of a troubling interview' *Cultural Studies* Vol. 4, No. 1: 61–84

TREACHER, Amal (1988) 'What is life without my love: desire and romantic fiction', in Radstone, Susannah (1988) editor, *Sweet Dreams: Sexuality, Gender and Popular Fiction* London: Lawrence & Wishart.

WILSON, Elizabeth (1988) 'The counterfeit detective', in *Hallucinations: Life in the Post-Modern City* London: Radius.

YOUNG, Shelagh (1988) 'Feminism and the politics of power: whose gaze is it anyway?', in **Gamman** and **Marshment** (1988).

Beleaguered but determined:

Irish Women Writers in Irish

Mary N. Harris

FEMINIST REVIEW NO 51, AUTUMN 1995, pp. 26–40

Abstract

A growing number of Irish women have chosen to write in Irish for reasons varying from a desire to promote and preserve the Irish language to a belief that a marginalized language is an appropriate vehicle of expression for marginalized women. Their work explores aspects of womanhood relating to sexuality, relationships, motherhood and religion. Some feel hampered by the lack of female models. Until recent years there were few attempts on the part of women to explore the reality of women's lives through literature in Irish. The largely subordinate role played by women in literary matters as teachers, translators, and writers of children's literature reflected the position of women in Irish society since the achievement of independence in the 1920s. The work of earlier women poets has, for the most part, lain buried in manuscripts and is only recently being excavated by scholars.

The problems of writing for a limited audience have been partially overcome in recent years by increased production of dual-language books. The increase in translation has sparked off an intense controversy among the Irish language community, some of whom are concerned that both the style and content of writing in Irish are adversely influenced by the knowledge that the literature will be read largely in translation. Nevertheless, translation also has positive implications. Interest in women's literature is helping to break down the traditional barriers between Irish literature in Irish and in English. The isolation of Irish literature in Irish is further broken down by the fact that women writers in Irish and their critics operate in a wider international context of women's literature.

Keywords

Irish; Gaelic; women writers; translation; poets

> The writing is a matter of love, the kind I have been describing a sustaining through my veins and verbs of something infinitely precious, a stretching back along the road we have come, a stand here in the present among the outnumbered and beleaguered but determined survivors of Gaelic Ireland.
>
> (Jenkinson, 1991: 33–4)

As I write I have an inner choice, am I the last tribesman of a forgotten people turning his monoglot face to the wall alone to die, or am I some anonymous martyr of an early Church who never saw, could never see, the chapel in the catacombs flower into the gold and colour of the mosaic-lined basilica?

(Mhac an tSaoi, 1990b: 96–7)

I think I'm very lucky in being Irish because the Irish language wasn't industrialized or patriarchialized. And many things, including this idea of a deeper quality, this negative femininity, this Hag Energy, which is so painful to mankind, hasn't been wiped from our consciousness, as it is in most other cultures. Irish in the Irish context is the language of the Mothers, because everything that has been done to women has been done to Irish. It has been marginalized, its status has been taken from it, it has been reduced to the language of small farmers and fishermen, and yet it has survived and survived in extraordinary richness, but not necessarily in a literary form, rather a paraliterary form.

(Nuala Ní Dhomhnaill quoted in Wilson and Somerville-Arjat, 1990: 154)

In recent years a growing body of literature, particularly poetry, has been written in Irish by women. This literature explores aspects of womanhood relating to love, sexuality, motherhood, relationships, and religion. It discusses dilemmas ranging from the difficulty of combining motherhood with writing to the difficulty of explaining the pill to one's elderly father. This work has reached a wider audience through its inclusion, with translation, in anthologies of Irish poetry and anthologies of women's writing (Bolger, 1986; Kelly, 1988; Smyth, 1989; Donovan et al., 1994). This article investigates why women have chosen to write in Irish, what difficulties surround this choice and what the implications of this choice are for Irish literature.

This phenomenon of writing in Irish is all the more interesting as many writers and most of their readers are not native speakers of Irish. Surveys indicate that about 5 per cent of the population use Irish as their first or main language and a further 10 per cent use Irish regularly but less intensively in conversation or reading (Ó Coileáin, n.d.: xviii). In the heyday of the cultural revival of the late nineteenth and early twentieth centuries, interest in finding an authentic Irish voice led some writers, most notably Synge, to look to Hiberno-English, the authentic speech of most of the Irish population. Yet in the case of both sexes, the most outstanding examples of its literary use were by those of Anglo-Irish backgrounds for whom this form of language served to portray something exotic rather than provide an authentic voice for self-expression. Women such as Lady Gregory, Jane Barlow (daughter of the provost of Trinity College, Dublin) and Edith Somerville and Violet Martin, better known as Somerville and Ross, attempted to represent the speech and thought patterns of Irish

FEMINIST REVIEW NO 51, AUTUMN 1995

peasants. This form of language, however, never gained recognition as a national language. Early attempts to write in it were viewed with disdain. D. P. Moran, journalist and cultural commentator, described it as a 'hopeless half-way house', neither good English nor good Irish, but a sort of bastard lingo which grew in the no man's land between two authentic cultures (Kiberd, 1993: xvi). When found in creative writing or drama now, Hiberno-English is generally used in dialogue or for satirical purposes and tends to be associated with stupidity or cunning (Croghan, 1986: 260). The place of national language was reserved for the Irish language. The newly independent Irish Free State accorded Irish equal place with English as official languages in its constitution. The position of the language was upgraded in the 1937 Constitution which declared Irish the national language. This, however, reflected aspirations rather than reality.

Much store was set by the education system's perceived ability to produce a nation of fluent Irish speakers. The degree of compulsion involved in language learning has had a detrimental effect on attitudes towards the language in the past, but changes in this area have seen a softening of attitudes in recent years. Now considerable value is attached to the symbolic role of the Irish language in ethnic identification and as a cultural value in and of itself, but this is accompanied by a general pessimism regarding the language's future and a feeling that it is inappropriate in modern life. The reality is, however, that while almost three-quarters of a century later most Irish children learn Irish in primary and post-primary school, it is mainly from among those who attend the all-Irish schools or who stay in the system the longest and take the academically most challenging syllabus that highly competent active users of Irish emerge (Ó Coileáin, n.d: 82–3). The language has been, and continues to be – in spite of small projects in some working-class areas – largely the preserve of a small middle-class élite. The potential audience for literature in Irish is, therefore, very limited, and most writers need to be motivated by concerns other than the desire to reach a wide audience.

The origins of modern Irish literature in Irish lie in the late nineteenth and early twentieth century cultural revival with its agenda of cultural separatism. In the words of Douglas Hyde, 'I believe it is our Gaelic past, which, though the Irish race does not recognise it just at present, is really at the bottom of the Irish heart, and prevents us becoming citizens of the Empire' (Hyde, 1892: 80). The Gaelic League, founded in 1894 to preserve and promote Irish, was unusual in the public sphere in allowing women to play a significant part at a time when women were excluded from many other organizations. Nevertheless, although the Anglo-Irish literary Renaissance produced a number of women writers, few wrote in Irish.

When the independent Irish state embarked on a policy of actively promoting the language, the role of many women was one of service to the language through scholarship, translating works into Irish, teaching and writing works in Irish for children and teenagers. This was indicative of the role of many women, single, married and religious, in Irish society at the time, who devoted their energies to bringing up their own or educating others' children. Sinéad Ní Fhlannagáin – who taught Irish to and later married Eamon de Valera – trained as a primary school teacher, was an active member of the Gaelic League, wrote works in Irish and English, and produced many retellings or translations of fairy and folk tales (Owens Weekes, 1993: 97). Searlot Ní Dhunlaing, A. Ní Chnáimhín, Máire Ní Chinnéide and Mairéad Ní Ghráda were among others who wrote for children. Of these only Mairéad Ní Ghráda was to produce substantial work for adults also.

The small quantity of creative prose work, whether for adults or children, included works of a historic and patriotic nature and works relating to folklore and mythology. While a number of male translators of novels into Irish were also novelists themselves, a similar trend did not emerge among female translators. Prose writing by women was particularly scarce, and women's realist portrayal of woman's life a rarity. In her study of the short story in Irish between 1898 and 1940, Aisling Ní Dhonnchadha (1981) lists works by twenty-four authors, all male. Short stories by women published in the magazine *Comhar* in later decades are often so short that they hardly merit inclusion in the genre. Short stories by women frequently had male protagonists, and depicted women's lives indirectly. In his comprehensive study of the Irish language novel Alan Titley (1991) lists novels by just five women: Úna Ní Fhaircheallaigh's *Grádh agus crádh* (1901), *An Cneamhaire* (1903), Úna Bean Uí Dhiosca's *Cailín na gruaige doinne* (1932), Nóra Ní Shéaghdha's *Peats na Baintreabhaighe* (1945) and Siobhán Ní Shúilleabháin's *Ospidéal* (1980). It was left largely to male writers such as Liam O'Flaherty and Pádraic Ó Conaire to highlight the reality of women's lives with problems such as rape within marriage, matchmaking, emigration.

Poetry was better served. Áine Ní Fhoghludha (1880–1932) wrote poetry in traditional metres, dealing with nature, religion, patriotism. More substantial writers were Caitlín Maude (1941–82) singer, actress, teacher as well as poet, and Máire Mhac an tSaoi (1922–), Nuala Ní Dhomhnaill (1952–) and Rita Kelly (1953–), who continue to flourish, and these have been joined more recently by other women poets, so that it is now realistic to speak of a women's literature in Irish. While this still consists largely of poetry, the genre is being developed to express the real concerns of contemporary Irish women.

Many contemporary women writers have commented on their choice of Irish. Máire Mhac an tSaoi has spoken of writing poetry out of a sense of duty to preserve the language (Mhac an tSaoi, 1990a: 22). Contemplating the decline of the language she says, 'I find empirically that I cannot read any poetry in Irish nowadays without a searing pang of pain' and is determined to arrest the decline of Irish:

> It is a startling and disconcerting manifestation of the tenacity of ancestor-worship, the pious conviction that the dead generations suffer if their children consign them to silence. Having lived myself in the single-minded grip of this belief for more than sixty years, I am now content that the observance will continue, the work will survive the shipwreck of the way of life from which it sprung, the graves will not be left untended. There is no way that all this passion can perish from the face of the earth.

> (Mhac an tSaoi, 1988: 33)

Máire Mhac an tSaoi's comments have drawn a spirited response from fellow poet Biddy Jenkinson: 'She has draped a shroud over us and I am determined to wiggle out . . . I am not aware of writing in a "fast dying minority language"'. For Biddy Jenkinson Irish is a living language, the language of her household and friends, and given the thriving nature of Irish language schools she feels the next generation of Irish speakers is secure, and does not worship the ancestors, although their influence is sometimes 'wind blown pollen on the stigma of imagination' (Jenkinson, 1989: 80).

Nuala Ní Dhomhnaill grew up in the West Kerry *gaeltacht*. As a schoolchild she began writing poetry in English, but realizing that the whole underpinning of the poetry was Irish she switched to Irish (Wilson and Somerville-Arjat, 1990: 149). For her there is no choice of language: she finds she cannot write poetry in English (Ní Dhomhnaill, 1992: 18). She describes Irish as the language of the mothers – marginalized, denied status, but living on in extraordinary richness among ordinary people. In this her comments are reminiscent of those of Irish women writers in English such as Eavan Boland who claims that 'Womanhood and Irishness are metaphors for one another. There are resonances of humiliation, oppression and silence in both of them and I think you can understand one better by experiencing the other' (Wilson and Somerville-Arjat, 1990: 85) and Medbh McGuckian, who, commenting on the gaelicization of her name, has said 'some part of me is desperately seeking a spiritual reunion with my native, Irish-speaking, peasant, repressed and destroyed ancestors and ancestresses' (Wilson and Somerville-Arjat, 1990: 5). Oppression is not the only issue, however, and Ní Dhomhnaill sees in Irish a language free from the influences of industrialization and the modern patriarchy

(Wilson and Somerville-Arjat, 1990: 154).

For other writers, however, writing in Irish is less an ideological issue, more another facet of their communication, an extension of their repertoire. For poet Deirdre Brennan 'one language complements the other. As time goes on I feel it easier to express myself in both languages since both are an integral part of my whole person' (Owens Weekes, 1993: 54). Eithne Strong who has published a number of volumes in each language is a native Irish speaker. Máire Mhac an tSaoi had pointed out that Strong is an immensely sophisticated poet in English, while her Irish verse seems deliberately to eschew sophistication, and asks, 'Is it her rural childhood that struggles here to find expression?' (Mhac an tSaoi, 1990b: 100). While Strong loves Irish, she does not wish to be identified with nationalism:

> It is far more important to be a citizen of the world. I am interested in human beings and the business of living with people, and it doesn't matter to me whether they are Irish or Chinese. I see languages as communication and ultimately humanity is more important than culture.
>
> (Wilson and Somerville-Arjat, 1990: 113)

Communication with a wider readership has been facilitated in recent years by the decision on the part of the Arts Council in 1984 actively to encourage translation (Cronin, 1991: 15). Dual-language books have begun to appear and books dealing with women's writing include poetry in both English and translation. Poetry has been translated by the poets themselves – many of whom are native speakers of English – by scholars, and by other poets. While this has had the advantage of drawing the attention of a wider audience to the existence of writing in Irish, it has also sparked off an intense debate among the Irish literary community. The most outspoken rejection of translation comes from Biddy Jenkinson:

> I prefer not to be translated into English in Ireland. It is a small rude gesture to those who think that everything can be harvested and stored without loss in an English-speaking Ireland.
>
> If I were a corncrake I would feel no obligation to have my skin cured, my tarsi injected with formalin so that I could fill a museum shelf in a world that saw no need for my kind.
>
> (Jenkinson, 1991: 34)

She argues that recognition has little to do with writing poetry and that 'the prerogative exercised by society in bestowing praise and blame is interesting to the poet only in that it is an aspect of human social behaviour that may be bad for her health' (Jenkinson, 1991: 27).

Others have expressed fears that the translation process will adversely affect the recognition, content and style of poetry. Gréagóir Ó Dúill has argued that the fashion of translation into English is now so prevalent that untranslated Irish poets can achieve little reputation even within their own language community (Ó Dúill, 1993: 12). One might add to that the fact that poetry is more likely to be translated than prose, and that prose writers are therefore more likely to live in obscurity. Nollaig Mac Congáil suggests that works by those whose second language is Irish might be more likely to be translated because they are easier to translate than the works of native Irish speakers (Mac Congáil, 1992: 123). Others are concerned that poetry will seek to conform to the stereotypes in the minds of the English language community, and a number of writers have expressed concern at the use of folklore in this respect (Ó Dúill, 1993: 12; Ó Cearnaigh, 1993: 63–4). In fact only a few writers make extensive use of folklore in their work. Tomás Mac Siomóin sees gaelicization as part of a process of decolonization: 'We must create a freethinking, indigenous mind, and our medium for doing so must be the Irish language.' He fears that some are writing in Irish for an audience which will read them in translation. 'When one writes for another readership – and there are people currently writing in Irish for an audience other than that which will read their work in Irish – one moulds, consciously or unconsciously, one's writing and the set of one's mind around the stereotypes which the other readership finds acceptable' (Ó Cearnaigh, 1994: 63).

While these comments may contain elements of truth, they seem to be of little concern to women writers whose work appears in both languages, and who seem to move freely from one to the other. Eithne Strong writes in both languages and has translated her poetry in both directions. Rita Kelly writes in both English and Irish, and worked on translations with her husband, the late Eoghan Ó Tuairisc. Her work has been translated into German, Dutch and Italian. In eschewing the type of cultural autarchy advocated by Mac Siomóin, losses in linguistic purity may be compensated by literary vibrancy. Irish language writers cannot remain culturally isolated from the English-speaking world. In fact contemporary Irish poetry can be said to date from the late 1960s when students Nuala Ní Dhomhnaill, Michael Davitt, Diarmaid Ó Muirthile and Gabriel Rosenstock embraced the modern world through Kerry Irish. Peter Denman recalls that in that formative period of the late 1960s there were in fact two groups of student poets on campus in Cork – an Irish language group and an English language group, and the two took an active interest in each other's writings, participating in joint poetry readings. He suggests that the sooner writers in both languages come to be seen as contributing to a common heritage of Irish writing, the better for all (Denman, 1985: 42).

A more serious aspect of the translation question is the extent to which translation conveys the sense and style of the original. This is particularly problematic in the case of Nuala Ní Dhomhnaill whose work has been translated by many established English language poets. Douglas Sealy, translator and critic, has pointed to the difficulty of forming any clear impression of the writer of the original poems, and asks if Nuala Ní Dhomhnaill has 'the smart raciness of Muldoon . . . the clotted, verbal richness of McGuckian, the conversational bite of Carson, the ornate elaboration of Longley . . . has she got the bewildering variety of tone supplied by thirteen translators?' (Cronin, 1991: 23). Tomás Mac Siomóin suggests that some of Ní Dhomhnaill's poetry appeals to the stereotype that poetry in Irish should be folkloric, rooted in an inaccessible *gaeltacht* region (Ó Cearnaigh, 1993: 70). But whatever their appeal to a wider audience interested in the exotic, it is precisely the most 'folkloric' of Ní Dhomhnaill's poems that lose much of their impact in translation. Ní Dhomhnaill's own comments point to the rootedness of her themes in the language, and a difficulty in separating language from theme. For her the Irish language belongs to a very different, preindustrialized world which accommodated a primitive feminine hag energy lost in many other cultures. Thus the transition from Irish to English has produced enormous difficulty for Irish people: 'If you call Irish the sea and English the land, the rationality of the land which we have had to crawl up onto has been terribly painful' (Wilson and Somerville-Arjat, 1990: 55). The difficulty of conveying her fusion of Irish tradition and women's issues in another language is compounded where the translator is less familiar with current feminist thinking and psychoanalytical theory than she. A few examples will highlight these difficulties. The whimsical, uncontrollable woman from the fairy fort – a symbol used by Ní Dhomhnaill to denote the deeper level of the psyche – who wreaks havoc with a Black and Decker in 'An Crann', becomes 'a bright young thing' in Paul Muldoon's translation of the poem (Bolger, 1986: 114–7), and the psychic element is obscured. Her poem 'Parthenogenesis' (Bolger, 1986: 126–9) also presents problems: it tells the story of a woman who encountered a mysterious and frightening, if alluring, shadow while swimming and later gave birth to a child of the sea. This is followed by the startling comparison between the woman's fear on encountering the shadow and the Virgin's anxiety at the annunciation. The impact is diminished if the reader is unfamiliar with the style and theme of the first part of the poem. Many of the resonances of her poem 'Feeding a Child' embodying nursery rhymes, children's songs and alliterative phrases are lost even in Michael Hartnett's excellent translation (Kiberd and Fitzmaurice, 1991: 291–3).

The complexity of women's writing in Irish merits serious critical attention. There has sometimes been a reluctance to criticize adequately works written by women, and works in Irish. Irish women's writing in Irish has

FEMINIST REVIEW NO 51, AUTUMN 1995

been doubly insulated. Nevertheless, valuable work has been done in recent years by critics such as Máirín Nic Eoin, Máire Ní Annracháin, Bríona Nic Dhiarmada, Angela Bourke and Máire Mhac an tSaoi whose criticism is frequently in the context of women's writing elsewhere. This marks progress from the type of criticism exemplified by Séamas Mac Gabhann who, reviewing *Ospidéal* by Siobhán Ní Shúilleabháin, found fault with her characterization but concluded that Siobhán Ní Shúilleabháin and her publishers were to be thanked for making this interesting attempt available for the Irish language community (Mac Gabhann, 1981: 33).

One of the difficulties mentioned by both critics and poets is that of the missing role model. Here Irish language women poets work under a double disadvantage: a ruptured Irish language literary tradition and the paucity of women's writing in Irish. Nuala Ní Dhomhnaill in an article entitled 'What foremothers?' writes passionately of the proverbial contempt for women poets and their exclusion from the literary canon, epitomized in the poem of Seán Ó Ríordáin – undoubtedly one of the greatest twentieth-century Irish language poets – entitled 'Banfhile', 'female poet', in which he states that woman is poetry, not poet (Ní Dhomhnaill, 1992: 23–4). Women have traditionally been associated with 'keening' or lamenting the dead (although, as Angela Bourke (1991–2) points out, laments rightfully belong in the category of oral literature or performance rather than written literature) but little else in terms of literary creation.

There are two tragedies here: the undoubted reality that women have played a small part in literary composition and the fact that much of the part they did play has gone unnoticed and unpublished. This indicates the poor state of scholarship in this area. Many crucial questions go either unasked or half answered. Some anthologies of women's writing deal with literature either by or about women as if it didn't really matter which was the case. These include P. L. Henry's *Dánta Ban: Poems of Irish Women Early and Modern* which aims 'to bring together from the successive phases of Irish civilisation memorable poems in which women, or the female principle, figure, either as a potent cause of poetry, or in the working out of poems' (Henry, 1991: 7). A recent anthology of writing in English and translations from Irish to English, aims, according to one of its editors, to 'celebrate women in Irish writing' and has at its centre 'women's lives, from the earliest times to the present day' (Donovan *et al.*, 1994: xvii). Such collections offer little consolation to those in search of foremothers. Issues relating to women's education are also underworked.

This poor state of scholarship is particularly regrettable as was clear from work carried out in the late nineteenth and early twentieth centuries by Douglas Hyde, by the compilers of the Gaelic League manuscripts deposited in the National Library of Ireland and by the contributors to the *Irisleabhar na Gaedhilge: the Gaelic Journal* that women were involved in the composition and transmission of literature in Irish. In 1909 *Irisleabhar na Gaeilge* published an award-winning essay by Máire Ní Chinnéide on the subject of modern literature in Irish. A short study by Máire Ní Dhubhghaill, *Women in Ancient and Modern Ireland*, published in 1917, deals in part with the education of women in ancient Ireland, arguing that women, like their fellow countrymen, were highly cultured. Yet despite the interest shown in such matters in the early twentieth century, many of the issues relating to women and literature were not until recently followed up by serious scholarly investigation.

Happily much research is now underway to begin to answer some of our questions. References to women in manuscript catalogues are currently being examined by Máirín Ní Dhonnchadha.[1] This research will provide a valuable source of information on women's literary activity. For although published sources are few, a glance at manuscript catalogues reveals names of women as authors and occasionally participants in poetic conversations with male poets, as well as patrons or subjects of poetry. Manuscripts such as those in the National Library of Ireland, Royal Irish Academy, Maynooth and University College Cork, include poems ascribed to women such as Caitilín Dubh (currently the subject of research by Liam Ó Murchú), Caitilín Ní tSéacháin, Eilín Ní Eachíaruinn, Máire Ní Mhurchú, Muirnn Ní Shúilliobháin and Máire Nic Aliondain. According to a pencil note on manuscript 23 B 19 in the Royal Irish Academy, the poem 'Coilte glasa na Triucha' was composed by Máire Nic Aliondain 'under the name of her brother Patrick the younger and addressed to a young woman named McBride of Thornfield to whom he paid his addresses.' One wonders how many other poems were composed by women under others' names. Further research is required to investigate the possibility that women did in fact compose works of literature in earlier periods. The education of women in early, medieval and early modern Ireland also needs to be investigated. Already valuable work has been and is being carried out in these areas by scholars such as Máirín Ní Dhonnchadha, Máire Herbert, Muireann Ní Bhrolcháin and Bernadette Cunningham.

Although contemporary women poets may feel orphans in the literary world, some have succeeded remarkably well in rooting themselves in a recognizable tradition. The poetry of Nuala Ní Dhomhnaill and Máire Áine Nic Ghearailt is clearly rooted in the language of West Kerry. Biddy Jenkinson's work draws on an older literary tradition, sometimes using syllabic metres reminiscent of those of bardic poetry in the classical period (1200–*c*.1650), and her language and imagery reveal familiarity with literature of an earlier period. Many writers clearly see themselves as part of a long line of enthusiasts who have laboured to preserve the language and show a commitment to continue that work. Máire Ní Chuinn's poem in tribute to Siobhán Uí Néill (1993: 28) moves those of us who have the good fortune to know that inspiring teacher of Irish in London. On the dust jacket of her novel *Ospidéal* Siobhán Ní Shúilleabháin (1980) is quoted as suggesting that perhaps it is more necessary to provide enough reading material of every kind than to wait for the work of excellence. She describes her novel as light and readable, though also dealing with life, particularly women's lives. Writing for the young continues, with writers such as Máire Áine Nic Ghearailt, Clíodna Cussen, Muireann Ní Bhrolcháin and others. Biddy Jenkinson is probably not alone in viewing her writing as 'a matter of love, the kind I have been describing a sustaining though my veins and verbs of something infinitely precious', taking a stand here in the present among the 'outnumbered and beleaguered but determined survivors of Gaelic Ireland' (Jenkinson, 1991: 33–4).

Irish women's writing in Irish is curiously positioned in Irish culture, challenging existing categories. It is simultaneously 'trendy', as women's studies is considered trendy, and 'backward' in the sense that revisionist historians and cultural affairs commentators tend to view enthusiasm for the Irish language as a sign of unreconstructed nationalism. And the twin pillars of Irish identity, language and religion, are placed in opposition to each other by women who use the Irish language to challenge traditional Catholic views on sexuality. For others, however, Irish serves as a vehicle for expression of their spirituality. Women's writing reflects the variety of female experience.

The increase in Irish women's writings in Irish also has implications for the Irish literary canon. While women's literature in both languages has frequently been overlooked in the past, the artistic creativity and ingenuity of writers in Irish is difficult to ignore, and a new generation of assertive women will not allow it to be ignored. Irish literature in Irish is being brought out of isolation. This is not in itself new: Irish literature has always tended to absorb external literary influences and use them creatively. In the past, however, influences were sometimes seen as threatening an essentialist definition of Irish literature. This was epitomized in Seán Ó Ríordáin's reference to English, in relation to his work, as a 'striapach allúrach' a foreign harlot (Ó Ríordáin, 1967: 10). Irish literature has now moved beyond that mentality and is increasingly interested in international issues such as postcolonialism. Women's writing is undoubtedly the most striking example of the contemporary internationalization of literary themes in Irish. Much, although certainly not all, of women's writing in Irish deals with women's issues and is informed at least partly by an awareness of the women's movement outside Ireland. This is particularly the case in relation to Nuala Ní Dhomhnaill, who refers to Julia Kristeva in her poetry readings. Thus a group of Irish language writers is part of a broader 'imagined community', a literary community extending beyond Ireland, and literary criticism of their work also bears that wider context in mind.

The availability of poetry in Irish in anthologies of poetry in both English and Irish and the increased accessibility of poetry through translation, although not without drawbacks, are likely to increase awareness of the existence of Irish literature in Irish. Given that there is a reservoir of people with a passive knowledge of Irish (Ó Coileáin, n.d.: xviii), it is possible that interest may be aroused not only in women's writing but in Irish literature in general. Translation and the tendency of some women to write in both languages will also encourage the bridging of the gap between studies of literature in Irish and in English. Traditionally such studies were undertaken with little reference to each other, even in the case of writers who wrote in both languages, a tendency decried as absurd by Declan Kiberd (1993: 7, 10). Studies of women's literature should encourage the removal of this barrier and lead on to a more holistic approach to the study of Irish-produced literature, and revised definitions of 'Irish literature'.

From a perspective of Women's Studies, an examination of Irish women's writing in Irish reveals trends reflecting the position of women in Irish society in general: the burial of early unpublished achievements in manuscripts, now in the process of excavation; the service role of Irish women as teachers, translators and producers of children's reading through to the increased visibility of women in recent years with the development of a women's literature in Irish. Yet here, too, one needs to be wary of facile categorization. Irish women's literature in Irish is tremendously varied. What is emerging, as Máirín Nic Eoin has pointed out, is 'less a distinctive "woman's voice" and more a whole chorus of voices, each distinctive, individual and recognisable' (Nic Eoin, 1992: 8). As the group defies easy categorization, so do many of the individuals within it. Máire Mhac an tSaoi who described her earlier lyrics as set in Arcadia, later changed direction, in response to criticism, and began to write 'not in the persona of the archetypal woman of my imagination, although she was intensely real to me, but as myself, myself as perceived by society, middle-class, middle-aged, suburban.' In retrospect she feels that the Dublin housewife is as much a dramatic creation as the earlier rural colleen (Mhac an tSaoi, 1990a: 24). Some women appear to use Irish as an extension of their repertoire, others who feel marginalized as women feel an affinity with a marginalized language, yet others choose to write in Irish from a passionate belief in the value of Gaelic culture in the face of its evident decline. In rejecting a dominant language, all are exercising an important personal and cultural choice which defies current notions of usefulness, and in the

FEMINIST REVIEW NO 51, AUTUMN 1995

process helps keep alive an interest in a language which has served as a vehicle for literary expression of emotion for fourteen hundred years. In the words of Máire Mhac an tSaoi

> For like all great literary media, Irish is (was?) the voice of a universe, ensuring access to all the elements, including those of time and space, necessary to the survival of the human spirit. It was never a mere rural patois, or the artificial dialect of an elitist in-group, but rather a great cultural compendium, encompassing a considerable part of the historical identity of these islands (note the plural) which cannot be, or at all events is not, available through the increasingly homogenised world language that is English.
>
> (Mhac an tSaoi, 1990b: 96)

Notes

Mary N. Harris was born and grew up in Cork, Ireland. She studied at University College, Cork and Cambridge University. She has taught in Cork and the Caribbean and is now Senior Lecturer in Irish Studies at the University of North London where she lectures in Irish History, Irish language and Irish literature in Irish.

1 I am grateful to Dr Máirín Ní Dhonnchadha of the Dublin Institute of Advanced Studies for her generosity in sharing sources for research relating to women in medieval Irish literature.

References

BOLGER, Dermot (1986) editor, *An Tonn Gheal: The Bright Wave*, Dublin: Raven Arts.

BOURKE, Angela (1991–2) 'Performing – not writing' in *Graph* Vol. 11 (Winter): 28–31.

CROGHAN, Martin J. (1986) 'The brogue language as political discourse' in Harris, John, Little, David and Singleton, David (1986) editors, *Perspectives on the English language in Ireland* Dublin: CLCS, Trinity College, Dublin: 259–69.

CRONIN, Michael (1991) 'Babel's suburbs: Irish verse translation in the 1980s' in *Irish University Review* Vol. 21, No. 1 (Spring/Summer): 15–26.

DENMAN, Peter (1985) reviews in *Poetry Ireland Review* Vol. 14 (Autumn): 40–6.

DONOVAN, Katie, JEFFARES, A. Norman and KENNELLY, Brendan (1994) editors, *Ireland's Women: Writings Past and Present*, Dublin: Gill & Macmillan.

HENRY, P. L. (1991) *Dánta Ban: Poems of Irish Women Ancient and Modern* Dublin: Gill & Macmillan.

HYDE, Douglas (1892) From 'The necessity of de-anglicising Ireland' reprinted in Storey, Mark (1988) editor, *Poetry in Ireland Since 1800: A Source Book* London and New York: Routledge: 78–84.

JENKINSON, Biddy (1989) 'Máire Mhac an tSaoi: the clerisy and the folk (*P.I.R.* 24) – A Reply', in *Poetry Ireland Review* Vol. 25 (Spring): 80.

—— (1991) 'A letter to an editor' in *Irish University Review* Vol. 21, No. 1(Spring/ Summer): 33–4.

KELLY, A. A. (1988) *Pillars of the House: An Anthology of Verse by Irish Women from 1690 to the Present Day* Dublin: Wolfhound Press.

KIBERD, Declan (1993) *Synge and the Irish Language* (2nd edn) Basingstoke: Macmillan.

KIBERD, Declan and FITZMAURICE, Gabriel (1991) *An Crann faoi Bhláth: the Flowering Tree* Dublin: Wolfhound Press.

MHAC AN tSAOI, Máire (1988) 'The clerisy and the folk: a review of present-day verse in the Irish language on the occasion of the publication of *Innti* 11', in *Poetry Ireland Review* Vol. 24 (Winter): 33–5.

—— (1990a) 'At work: poet as housewife', in *Poetry Ireland Review* Vol. 28 (Spring): 22–4.

—— (1990b) 'Minority culture', in *Poetry Ireland Review* Vol. 30 (Autumn/ Winter): 96–101.

MAC CONGÁIL, Nollaig (1992) 'Nua-litríocht na Gaeilge i bhfoirm Aistriúcháin', in *Irisleabhar Mhá Nuad*: 123–33.

MAC GABHANN, Séamas (1981) review of *Ospidéal* by Siobhán Ní Shúilleabháin in *Comhar* Vol. 40, No. 10 (October): 32–3.

NIC EOIN, Máirín (1992) 'Gender's agendas', in *Graph* Vol. 12 (Summer/ Autumn): 5–8.

NÍ CHINNÉIDE, Máire (1909) 'Nuadh-litridheacht na nGaodhal', in *Irisleabhar na Gaedhilge* Vol. 19: 610–8 and Vol. 20: 73–80.

NÍ CHUINN, Máire (1993) *Eala ar an Uisce* London: Approach.

NÍ DHOMHNAILL, Nuala (1992) 'What foremothers?' in *Poetry Ireland Review* Vol. 36 (Autumn): 18–31.

NÍ DHONNCHADHA, Aisling (1981) *An Gearrscéal sa Ghaeilge 1898–1940* Dublin: An Clóchomhar.

NÍ DHUBHGHAILL, Máire (1917) *Women in Ancient and Modern Ireland* Dublin: Kenny Press.

NÍ SHÚILLEABHÁIN, Siobhán (1980) *Ospidéal* Dublin: Foilseacháin Náisiúnta Teoranta.

Ó CEARNAIGH, Seán (chair) (1993) 'Debate: thoughts on translation', in *Poetry Ireland Review* Vol. 39 (Autumn): 61–72.

Ó COILEÁIN, Antoine (n.d.) editor, *The Irish Language in a Changing Society* Dublin: Bord na Gaeilge.

Ó DÚILL, Gréagóir (1993) 'Infinite grounds for hope? Poetry in Irish today', in *Poetry Ireland Review* Vol. 39 (Autumn): 9–27.

Ó RÍORDÁIN, Seán (1967) *Brosna* Dublin: Sairséal agus Dill.

OWENS WEEKES, Ann (1993) *Unveiling Treasures: The Attic Guide to the Published Works of Irish Women Literary Writers* Dublin: Attic.

SMYTH, Ailbhe (1989) editor, *Wildish Things: An Anthology of New Irish Women's Writing* Dublin: Attic Press.

TITLEY, Alan (1991) *An tÚrscéal Gaeilge* Dublin: An Clóchomhar.

WILSON, Rebecca E. and **SOMERVILLE-ARJAT, Gillean** (1990) *Sleeping with Monsters: Conversations with Scottish and Irish Women Poets* Edinburgh: Polygon.

'Great Expectations':
Rehabilitating the Recalcitrant War Poets

Gill Plain

FEMINIST REVIEW NO 51, AUTUMN 1995, PP. 41–65

Abstract

Formulating a definition of 'good' poetry is, and should be, impossible. Yet women's poetry of the First World War seems generally to have been condemned as 'bad'. It inspires an ambiguous response from readers who recognize the value of its historical, social and psychological content, but shudder at the limitations of its form. However, I believe that a much more fruitful reading of these 'recalcitrant' texts is possible. It is not my intention to deny either their problematic nature, or the diversity and complexity of male responses to the war, but rather to emphasize that women's experience of the First World War was radically different from that of men, and we should not therefore be constrained by the traditional parameters of 1914–18 criticism when we explore these works. This article examines a selection of this poetry in the light of the psychological processes of grief and bereavement, and in so doing indicates other areas in which constructive readings of these texts might be made.

Why do we expect the articulation of a radically new and uniformly consistent poetic voice from what was a large and diverse group of women? The expectations of modernism ironically have created a literary 'mainstream' out of a selection of experimental, and largely male, writing. I hope to show that the 'failure' of these women to conform to our textual 'great expectations' is irrelevant. The single most characteristic feature of these women's experience of war was isolation. Their position had neither the homogeneity of the trenches, nor the intense intellectualism of experimental circles. Predominantly middle class, alienated by absence and bereavement, they attempted to articulate the unprecedented nature of their experience. That their experiments were not wholly successful is perhaps indicative of the near impossibility of the task they undertook.

Keywords

poetry; women; First World War; Kristeva; grief-work

> A distinction should be made between two groups – those who themselves risk their lives in battle, and those who have stayed at home and have only to wait for the loss of one of their dear ones by wounds, disease or infection.

> (Freud, 1915: 291)

FEMINIST REVIEW NO 51, AUTUMN 1995

It might be said that we owe the fairest flowerings of our love to the reaction against the hostile impulse which we sense within us.

(Freud, 1915: 299)

Women's poetry of the First World War, returning to critical attention after a sixty-year exile in the no man's land of canonical exclusion, has been greeted more with alarm than enthusiasm. Commentators seem mostly to agree that at best this work is problematic, at worst, embarrassing. Catherine Reilly's bibliographical work has uncovered 532 published women poets from this period, nearly all of whom have since been forgotten. Reilly's anthology, *Scars Upon My Heart* (1981), aims to provide a representative selection, and resists the temptation to pass judgement on the poets, whose work can fairly be said to run the gamut from the sublime to the distressing. Part of the problem in approaching this body of work would seem to lie in the critical status of war poetry in general – as Susan Schweik (1987: 310) has indicated, an anxiety of authenticity surrounds the written response to all the major conflicts of the twentieth century. However, from the midst of the debates these 500-plus women emerge as particularly troublesome poets. Lacking the superficial homogeneity of the soldier-poets' experience of life in the trenches, or even a cohesive vision of life on the home front, these disparate writers stubbornly resist comfortable categorization as chroniclers, defenders or even supporters of the conflict.

There seems, in the brief history of these writers' resurrection from obscurity, to be a critical tension evident between the excitement of discovering women's writing and the disappointment that can follow when it fails to turn out as hoped. Even positive responses are followed by confusion over what to do with a body of literature that refuses to conform to any coherent literary or political framework. Nosheen Khan's (1989) attempt to tackle the problem in her *Women's Poetry of the First World War* is impressive in scope, but its impact is diffused by the constant search for influence it undertakes. We are told of the similarities between Margaret Sackville's 'The Dead' and Owen's 'Anthem for Doomed Youth' (Khan, 1989: 31), while Constance Ada Renshaw's 'All Quiet on the Western Front' is compared to Owen's later 'Exposure' (1989: 22). Women, we are told, 'were writing protest poetry before Sassoon and Owen' (1989: 15). While it is encouraging to realize that women's response to war cannot be dismissed as a tapestry of second-hand images gleaned from the 'reality' of masculine experience, I believe that comparisons of this sort are ultimately unsatisfactory and contribute little to our understanding of the disparate façades presented by women's war poetry. Khan's work seems more successful when she focuses on difference, on the factors that divide rather than unite gendered responses to war:

The claim that war makes upon women is, in comparison with that made upon men, more hidden and often more difficult; for it is easier to be active than passive, easier to place oneself under obedience in a time of crisis than to serve by silent anxiety. Courage is manifest not only in brilliant attack, but also in patient waiting and patient endurance.

(Khan, 1989: 138)

Perhaps the problem presented by these poets is the same one that haunts Susan Schweik in her study of Marianne Moore (Schweik, 1987: 312). How can a war poem survive the imposition of 'a familiar set of post-war aesthetic values'? Discussing Moore's 'In Distrust of Merits' (canonized by one generation – excommunicated by the next) Schweik suggests the poem has fallen victim to attempts at a definition of aesthetic merit:

A good poem – that is, a poem unpressured, or pressured just enough – will be cleanly universal and timeless, where "In Distrust" bears too obviously the imprints of an immediate historical and cultural context; it will be neutral, where "In Distrust" is polemical; it will enact poetically, where "In Distrust" spouts off oratorically; it will address an elite readership, where "In Distrust" invites the same kind of attention as the *Saturday Evening Post*.

(Showalter, 1989: 312–13)

Schweik's irony indicates the futility of pursuing the chimera of 'good' poetry. It is not simply a matter of the impossibility of establishing criteria for such a definition; to consider this work only upon the grounds of artistic value is to ignore the many provocative questions it raises not just for the social historian but also for the literary critic.

There is, I would argue, a need to revise the frames of reference within which we consider these writers. A number of recent critics, notably Clare Tylee (1990) and Sharon Ouditt (1994), have tackled the impact of the First World War on women through examining fiction, diaries and memoirs. Ouditt's *Fighting Forces, Writing Women* is an excellent examination of the contradictory ideological forces that operated on women before, during and after the war which, while acknowledging the lack of homogeneity that characterizes women's writing, none the less does much to establish the parameters within which women could formulate their responses to the conflict.

In war the act of writing is potentially as significant as what is actually written. A poem's explicit content, the form that conveys that content, and the tensions that may exist between the two, create an arena for the articulation of a plethora of implicit possibilities. The writing and publishing of poetry constitute an engagement with the act and ideology of war that is not private but public. It is all too easy to forget that in the years of the First World War, poetry had an audience. It was produced and

FEMINIST REVIEW NO 51, AUTUMN 1995

consumed by a voracious public who both shaped and were shaped by the verse they read. In consequence I would like to suggest a shift in critical attention from what women wrote to the (f)act of their writing. This transition raises two significant questions. Why did women write in wartime and why was this writing effaced from the record of war? To the first question I would answer that many wrote as a part of the work of mourning; they produced a poetry of grief that encodes not just the pain of personal loss but also the politics of personal identity. The second question is both a mystery and a case of *déjà vu* that this article cannot hope to resolve. None the less I believe that a consideration of women's mourning as a subversive act may cast helpful light upon the case of the recalcitrant war poets, and that by connecting theories of women's subjectivity with the psychological study of grief and bereavement, we can see these diverse poetic fragments as complex articulations of war's paradoxical emancipation and repression of women.

The dominant images of the First World War into which this poetry refuses to fit are founded on a particular version of masculine experience, just as the literary categories it eludes have been defined by men. The social, political, legal and economic status of women in 1914 was such as to leave women almost no grounds for connection with the masculine arena. The energetic suffrage activity that preceded the conflict was not something that could be translated into a single unified female response to the fact of war. War creates its own terms and they are quite unlike the conditions of peace. These poems, like the enormously diverse range of male voices from the period, are the products of an intellectual and emotional economy of war, and in war nothing is ever quite the same. The writers explored in Ouditt's work and the poets of Reilly's anthology describe a paradoxical intensification of experience that is only partly related to changing work patterns. Daily life was transformed by absences, shortages, and above all by the rhetoric of patriotism – which effectively legitimizes the repression of internal debate and dissent in the name of national security – the claim that 'we must all pull together for the duration'. As late as 1918 readers of anthologies such as Theodora Thompson's *The Coming Dawn* were being told that:

> [t]errible as the suffering and sacrifice are which war involves, we should surely be able to see that it is in humanity's name that we are destroying humanity . . . We are too apt to allow the apparent tragedy of it all to obscure the great spiritual significance – the wonderful manifestation of national unity.
>
> (Thompson, 1918: xiii–xiv)

Historians and literary critics have debated the extent of the transformation war wrought on British society. Amongst those analysing women's writing, Sandra Gilbert (1983: 200) has argued that a remarkable sense of female liberation emerged from the conflict, while Sharon Ouditt (1994: chapter 1) offers a more restrained reading that suggests simply an element of emancipation in the wartime work experiences of women. Historians, meanwhile, have debated the idea of a 'lost generation' and the associated perception of a somehow impoverished post-war world. J. M. Winter contends that the lost generation was more of a myth than a reality, and statistically speaking this would seem to be the case (1981: 256–63). A. J. P. Taylor observes that 'the slaughter of war was less than the loss by emigration', but goes on to conclude that '[t]hough the death roll was not large enough to create statistically a "lost generation", there may have been an exaggerated sense of loss amongst those who survived' (1965/92: 120–1). Cannadine agrees with this distinction and argues that whether there was a 'demographic disaster' or not, the important fact was that people believed in one (1981: 200–1). It would be a mistake to underestimate the power of such myths in shaping responses to the war. It is also important to consider the distribution of actual losses across the classes. Taylor points out that 'Casualties were about three times heavier in proportion among junior officers than with common soldiers' (1965/92: 120) – a factor which cannot be ignored in the study of a body of women's poetry which is almost exclusively middle class. Irrespective of statistics for the country as a whole, for the middle-class women who struggled to write war poetry in this period, both the perception and the actuality of loss would have been significant.

Early twentieth-century gender politics add an extra dimension to this dislocation. Ouditt observes that war is 'isolating and annihilating for women who live their lives through their men and who then lose their entire investment' (1994: 125), a comment which raises significant questions about the precarious nature of female subjectivity. If women are encouraged to live their lives through and for their men, what happens when those men are removed? Are the women who stay behind left to exist in a vacuum, do they go into some form of existential cold storage until their plucky soldier-boys come marching back? Or do they begin the slow process of formulating an identity in which the absence of the subject to which they are other gives them an unprecedented degree of mobility within the constraints of the symbolic order? These questions beg others.

The impact of war on women's lives is inevitably mediated through the ideologies and institutions of English class society. The opportunities open to women for a public redefinition of their subjectivity were controlled by the demands not only of the war machine, but also of a class hierarchy determined to maintain the status quo. To a large extent the public father of institutional organization, be it in the ranks of the VAD or in the munitions factories, took over the role left vacant by the absence of the domestic male. Women's access to the public sphere was only for the duration, and Ouditt indicates how damage limitation measures were undertaken by the authorities to ensure that any revolutionary potential inherent in this gender disruption was strangled at birth. The organization of the VAD, 'precariously constructed upon aspirations towards militarism and equality' was, claims Ouditt, 'consistently undermined by the conservative pressures of class and gendered identity' (1994: 16). The demands of femininity were deployed to enforce women's continued conformity and a cycle was perpetuated whereby 'the ideological structures that ensured these women their ticket out to the war, equally ensured that they made a round trip' (1994: 30).

The arena of women's public redefinition was, then, necessarily constrained. But these limitations could not apply to the same extent to women's private exploration of a new subjectivity – however much the women's magazines of the period fought to impose upon their readership the moral duty of uncomplaining self-sacrifice. Within the fragmentary and diffuse body of women's war poetry there is an articulation of these changes in women's sense of self, and these changes gained access to the margins of the public sphere through the act of publication. The extent of the poetry's readership is hard to gauge, but whether these works were ignored or applauded, they provide fascinating information for a study of the ways in which women survive war. In order to explore women's relation to the contending logics of war, I will be using Julia Kristeva's terminology of the semiotic and the symbolic, by which I understand a distinction between the dominant order of language that constructs our identity (the symbolic) and the elements that must be repressed in order to maintain or enter that order (the semiotic). Kristeva uses the term semiotic to refer to the pre-Oedipal stage of child development, the period in which the child knows no boundaries and has no sense of itself as an independent social or gendered being. She also theorizes a revolutionary potential within this chora of repressed drives. These constantly fluctuating forces are never fully silenced by the symbolic order, but exist in parallel, or beneath the surface, to return as irruptions and dislocations that have the power to destabilize and disrupt that order. Women are marginal to the symbolic order. They exist on the periphery and are faced with a choice between a masculine identification, which includes that deriving of a sense of self through a husband or father, as described above, or a feminine identification that leaves them outside the arena of power, if not without a voice, then certainly without an audience!

I would like, then, to situate women's war poetry within an exploration of female subjectivity, and the focalizer I shall use for this purpose is the study of grief. Grief can be described as the manifestation of loss. Usually considered as the affect of a private trauma, it also has the potential to assume a public dimension. This wider significance becomes evident in Sharon Ouditt's examination of the reactionary ideology that characterized many women's magazines of the period. From this analysis she draws a fascinating and disturbing conclusion:

> In one of *Woman's World*'s 'Heart to Heart Chats' the editress replies rather impatiently to a reader who has already lost three children and whose husband has now gone to France:
>
>> Dear sister, I am so sorry to hear of your unhappiness. But, dearie, you must really try to be more cheerful, and face the separation from your husband a little more bravely. . . . (*Woman's World* 15 May 1915: 540)
>
> The appellation 'dearie' creates an atmosphere of (false) intimacy, within which it can be clearly intimated that revealing one's unhappiness is unpatriotic.
>
> (Ouditt, 1994: 95)

Revealing one's unhappiness is unpatriotic.[1] And yet, whether it is manifested in an 'ecstacy' of sacrifice, or in religious sublimation, or a total revulsion from the futility of war, grief and loss form the dominant tone of Reilly's anthology. If misery is unpatriotic, then the collected grief within *Scars Upon My Heart* has the potential to form a revolutionary text!

This suggestion is not as improbable as it may at first sound. Individual grief may be powerless to effect political change, but collective grief would seem to have embodied a sufficiently threatening force to intimidate Britain's post-war government. In a fascinating article on the changing patterns of mourning in Britain, David Cannadine describes the government's reluctance to institute both the ritual of Armistice Day and the Cenotaph monument. Lord Curzon, chairman of the committee established to organize the national post-war rejoicing, was 'distinctly unenthusiastic' about Lloyd George's proposal for a war memorial. The plan was put before the committee who proved to share Curzon's doubts:

> The reasons against the proposal were: that it was foreign to the customs and temper of the nation; that it might not be easy for the public to assume the properly reverential attitude; and, as the structure would be of a very temporary character, it must be carefully safeguarded or it would be overturned and trampled in the crush.
>
> (Quoted in Cannadine, 1981: 220)

There seems to be a genuine fear of the extent of public grief, and of the potential force of its expression. The anxiety of a ruling class that feels its position has been undermined by the socially disruptive events of the previous four years, is combined with a xenophobia that would deploy the convenient myth of British reserve as a means of repressing the outburst of public feeling occasioned by the war. These anxieties were not without foundation. Much of Cannadine's article is concerned with the difficulty of maintaining pre-war standards of outward mourning in the face of such an unprecedented excess of death. He observes that the conditions of the battlefield exacerbated the impossibility of paying due respect, resulting often in the adoption of a protective cynicism, which would have contributed to the more general perception of a post-war breakdown in traditional patterns of deference based on age and class. This disruption, in which the working classes were increasingly revealed not to know their place, is evident from before the end of the conflict. In Gilbert Stone's 1917 anthology *Women War Workers*, an interview with a female bus conductor 'the majority of . . . [whom] . . . have undoubtedly been drawn from the ranks of better-class domestic servants' (1917: 112), reveals both interviewer and interviewee's anxiety about the probable reluctance of women to leave the freedom of outside employment for the underpaid constraints of domestic service.

None the less, the plans for both Cenotaph and Armistice Day went ahead and proved to be enormously popular, which ensured that they became permanent rather than temporary legacies of the nation's loss. The extent of the public response suggests that there existed a huge desire for the legitimization of their individual and collective grief. However, the government need not have worried that these monuments would become sites of disaffection. Cannadine concludes that the popularity of the rituals lay in their capacity to make 'public and corporate those unassuageable feelings of grief and sorrow which otherwise must remain forever private and individual' (Cannadine, 1981: 222).[2] The idea of incorporation ultimately suggests a ritual appropriated by patriarchal authority rather than a show of opposition or resistance to that authority, but it is none the less interesting to note that momentary hesitation on the part of those in power.[3]

How, then, does this body of poetry engage with grief? Psychoanalytic theorists from Freud to Kristeva, in an attempt to explore the melancholic condition, have given considerable thought to defining its close relation, the so called 'normal' process of mourning. In 'Mourning and Melancholia' Freud describes the relation between the two conditions:

> Profound mourning, the reaction to the loss of someone who is loved, contains the same painful frame of mind, the same loss of interest in the outside world – in so far as it does not recall him – the same loss of capacity to adopt any new

object of love (which would mean replacing him) and the same turning away from any activity that is not connected with thoughts of him [as is witnessed in melancholia].

(Freud, 1917: 244)

In this state, the ego is inhibited and circumscribed by its 'exclusive devotion to mourning' (Freud, 1917: 244), and the gradual recovery from this position is achieved through a process described by Freud as 'reality-testing'. The memories of the past are juxtaposed against the actuality of the present until it becomes possible for the bereaved to acknowledge the absence of the loved object:

This demand arouses understandable opposition . . . [which] . . . can be so intense that a turning away from reality takes place and a clinging to the object through the medium of a hallucinatory wishful psychosis. Normally, respect for reality gains the day. Nevertheless its orders cannot be obeyed at once. They are carried out bit by bit, at great expense of time and cathectic energy, and in the meantime the existence of the lost object is psychically prolonged. Each single one of the memories and expectations in which the libido is bound to the object is brought up and hyper-cathected and detachment of the libido is accomplished in respect of it.

(Freud, 1917: 244–5)

This process is evident in the considerable number of wartime and post-war poems that revisit places previously shared with a lost lover, or which focus on an activity or ideal associated with the lost person. I will consider the manifestations of the mourning process in some detail later, but Freud's observations can be aptly illustrated by Eileen Newton's poem 'Revision (For November 11th)'. Newton refuses reality, she will not dwell on 'the untimely slain', preferring instead to let her thoughts seek 'a hallowed place –/ The little, leafy wood where you and I/ Spent the last hour together' (Reilly, 1981: 81–2). It is also interesting to consider Anna Gordon Keown's 'Reported Missing', a poem which operates within a state of limbo that could be described as pre-bereavement. Keown's sonnet redirects the operation of reality-testing, turning it into an act of defiance, a statement of presence that covers the unacknowledgable fact of absence:

Of these familiar things I have no dread
Being so very sure you are not dead.

(Reilly, 1981: 58)

The work of mourning is a burden, its painfulness evident in the tension between the desire to remember and the instinct to survive that demands that we forget. 'Who shall deliver us from the memory of these dead?' cries Margaret Sackville in 'A Memory' (Reilly, 1981: 95), indicating the intense difficulty of freeing oneself even from a past that imprisons. This difficulty is particularly evident in the work of Vera Brittain, the immensity of whose loss gives rise to a sense of total, debilitating exhaustion:

SIC TRANSIT –
(V. R., Died of Wounds, 2nd London General Hospital,
Chelsea, June 9th, 1917)

I am so tired.
    The dying sun incarnadines the west,
And every window with its gold is fired;
    And all I loved the best
Is gone, and every good that I desired
    Passes away, an idle hopeless quest;
Even the highest whereto I aspired
    Has vanished with the rest.
I am so tired.

London,
    June, 1917

(Brittain, 1918)

Brittain, like many of the poets in Reilly's anthology, juxtaposes short monosyllabic lines against heavier Latinate syntax in what can be seen as an attempt, through formal experiment, to augment the sense of fragmentation and dislocation already contained within the content of the poems. For these women poets, as well as for their contemporaries in the trenches and in artistic circles, there was a need to challenge outmoded and overly restrictive poetic forms which seemed inadequate to express the unprecedented carnage of the war. The opening of 'Sic Transit', however, achieves considerable impact through its extreme simplicity, and the repetition of this line at the end of the poem reinforces the contrast between the poem's central 'elevated' or poetic diction, and the reality of exhaustion. 'I am so tired' forms a frame for the polysyllabic outburst that provides the substance of the verse. The seven lines within this frame are laden with images of death and finality. 'Incarnadines', apart from meaning to dye flesh-coloured or crimson, has its roots in Shakespeare's Macbeth:

Will all great Neptune's ocean wash this blood
Clean from my hand? No; this my hand will rather
The multitudinous seas incarnadine,
Making the green one red.

(II, ii. 59–62)

Brittain's imagery evokes blood and wholesale, gratuitous slaughter from motives of greed and ambition. The window which is fired with gold not only represents the closure of sunset, symbolic of an end to youth, hope, and life, it also evokes an image of 'stained' glass.

The irregularity of the poem's stress pattern also works to create the overriding impression of weariness and despair. The contextually hopeful open-ended line 'And all I loved the best' rises in pitch before receiving its sense conclusion in the flat beginning of the next line with the simple words 'Is gone'. The rhythm that is created in this phrase is echoed in the following four lines, gradually and inexorably turning this short poem into one in which hopes and happiness are destroyed with an exhausting regularity before the reader is returned to the concluding and inevitable statement, 'I am so tired'.

Brittain's alternation in this poem between exhaustion and intensity can be related to the psychologist Colin Murray Parkes's anatomy of the process of grief. In his book *Bereavement* he describes alternating patterns of anger and passivity as a characteristic phase of grief, alongside avoidance, postponement, searching, self-reproach and 'the gradual building-up of a fresh identity' (1972/86: 12). There are elements of all these factors present in the poetry of the war, but perhaps the most important is the search component, which Parkes suggests is unique to the experience of bereavement. The act of searching takes many forms, all of which can be seen in the poetry of Brittain. For example, her poem 'Roundel ("Died of Wounds")' begins:

> Because you died, I shall not rest again,
>   But wander ever through the lone world wide,
> Seeking the shadow of a dream grown vain
>   Because you died.

(Brittain, 1918)

But searching is more complex than this restlessness might suggest. Parkes observes that the bereaved often develop a fresh attachment to items or people of whom the deceased was particularly fond – a phenomenon that can do much to explain why so many women were able to maintain a belief in the war that had killed their husbands, sons or lovers. Particularly in the early years of the conflict, women whose menfolk departed for battle imbued with a noble spirit of love for their country, continued to believe in the necessity of the war. Aside from the obvious need to give a purpose to an otherwise futile death (the process of 'making sense' that Freud terms 'grief work'), this can be seen as a desire to 'keep faith' with the dead, which in turn enables the preservation or restoration of some part of the person who has been lost. May Wedderburn Cannan's poem 'After' encapsulates this dynamic:

Dear, since it was for England that you died
Who so adored her, I will love her still;

(Cannan, 1919: 33)

Cannan is more self-conscious than most, but her comment is typical of a need for belief, or for explanation, that accompanied the moral vacuum of war. At its worst this need for some sort of answer is manifested in the prescription poetry of Katharine Tynan, who dispensed the consolation of her religion to readers in need of comfort. Her poem 'To the Others' reveals her tendency to view the war as some form of religious crusade in which all those participating will receive an indulgence:

Your son and my son, clean as new swords,
Your man and my man and now the lord's!
Your son and my son for the great crusade,
With the banner of Christ over them – our knights, new-made.

(Tynan, 1916: 16)

Tynan believed that the war was being fought in a good cause, and that all soldiers, particularly dead ones, were necessarily heroic.[4] This belief was accompanied by the idea, encouraged by the poster art of the period, that those who sacrificed a loved one to the cause were equally heroic. Acceptance of this dubious consolation was perhaps one of the more conservative strategies that women employed in the process of surviving grief. However, not all the poems which manifest religion as a coping strategy are as straightforward as those of Katharine Tynan. Violet Spender's 'Forever and Forever', provides an example of this complexity. The poem reinforces the association of unhappiness with treachery by suggesting despair to be the devil incarnate. The sinister implications of this characterization are, however, somewhat undermined by the voice of despair's Raven-like repetition of 'Nevermore!'. What is curious about Spender's poems is not the patriotic line that they ultimately take, but the time and effort she devotes to the delineation of doubt, anxiety and the very 'unpatriotic' feelings she protests to abhor. Far removed as her poetry is from that of Milton, she suffers, it would seem, from a tendency to make the devil's part the more convincing:

But when his friends had bidden her farewell
And all the letters had been laid aside,
She heard a voice that whispered in her ear:
'He was a hero; but he lives no more!
You may now listen, listen for his tread,
But he will never, never come again! . . .

"But he will never, never come again
Your daily plans and pleasures! Never more!

Figure 1 Recruiting poster no. 75. Crown copyright.

The dreams, the hopes, the visions! Faded! Fled!
The Future? Music ended! Lights put out!
And is there any sound in all the world
But Never! Never! Never any more?"

(Spender, 1922: 47)

The constant repetition of 'never', while not a sophisticated expression of her emotions, none the less contains considerably more vigour than the pallid expression of piety that follows it:

And then she rose up stronger and she cried:
"Go from me! Now I know you! For you are
The Devil who would slay the soul of me
And murder my good deeds ere they be born
By showing them the visage of Despair
Which turns to stone all those that look on her.
I know that he will never come again;
But God be praised because he came at all!"

(Spender, 1922: 47)

This can be read, as Jan Montefiore reads Macaulay's 'Picnic' (Montefiore, 1993: 61), more as a defence against emotional collapse than a genuine belief in the clichéd consolation that it is better to have loved and lost than never to have loved at all.[5]

Returning to the work of May Cannan, however, it is interesting to note the direct address to the dead used at the beginning of 'After' – a technique which also characterizes her poem 'Fulfilment':

Dear, since you've gone across the other side
(Beyond the stars, men say), you'll wait for me
Who only wish I also could have died,

(Cannan, 1919: 30)

This is not only typical of Cannan's poetry, it is also connected to another crucial grief phenomenon. Parkes suggests that 'the commonest means of mitigating the pain of grieving comprises the maintenance of a feeling or impression that the bereaved person is nearby although they may not be seen or heard' (1972/86: 77). This pattern is evident in Mary Boyle's *Aftermath* (1916), which the poet described as a 'private memorial' to the brother she lost in 1914. *Aftermath* openly acknowledges its status as grief work; in her preface to the sequence of thirty sonnets Boyle claims they were written 'not as a literary exercise, but in remembrance'. The poems themselves comprise a psychological battle between the reality-testing of 'trait'rous memory's stabbing knives' (Sonnet II) and the comforting belief in her brother's ghostly presence:

You entered with your face of radiant morn,
And kneeling, whispered, 'Dearest, I've come home.'

(Sonnet I)

Sometimes I hear your footstep on the stair,
A curious way you scuffled slippered feet,
And am inclined to run halfway and meet
You on my threshold.

(Sonnet V)

Boyle is not alone in her desire to recreate the lost object of her love – indeed, the ghosts of the war dead people the pages of Reilly's anthology: 'I hear you laughing as you used to do' (Marian Allen in Reilly, 1981: 1), 'Now in the quiet of a chill Winter's night/ Your voice comes hushed to me' (Cannan/Reilly, 1981: 16), '. . . yet your feet/ Pass with the others down the twilit street' (Nora Griffiths/Reilly, 1981: 44). Many more of the poems are simply addressed to the dead – the articulated half of an impossible dialogue.

Grief, then, is an integral component of this body of poetry – but what psychological function does the creative process serve? Freud's idea of 'grief work' can perhaps provide an answer. In *Testament of Youth*, Vera Brittain describes an almost physical need to write poetry:

and all at once the impulse to put what I felt into verse – a new impulse which had recently begun to fascinate and torment me – sprang up with overwhelming compulsion.

(Brittain, 1933/78: 268)

Brittain's sentiment is endorsed by the imagist poet Marianne Moore, who suggests that 'one writes because one has a burning desire to objectify what is indispensable to one's happiness to express' (Jones, 1972: 38). The act of writing a grief poem involves the transforming of a painful amorphous emotion into a concrete form, with a solid, repeatable shape. The poem metamorphoses the grief into a more finite entity – in effect it creates a monument. As a monument the poem can bear witness to both the loss and the grief, while at the same time placing it outside – at a distance from the poet. By providing at least a temporary detachment from the emotion that provoked the urge to write, the poem assumes a cathartic function. Eleanor Farjeon's poem 'The Outlet' embodies this idea:

Grief struck me. I so shook in heart and wit
I thought I must speak of it or die of it.

A certain friend I had with strength to lend,
When mine was spent I went to find my friend,

Who, rising up with eyes wild for relief,
Hung on my neck and spoke to me of grief.

I raked the ashes of my burned-out strength
And found one coal to warm her with at length.

I sat with her till I was icy cold.
At last I went away, my grief untold.

(Farjeon, 1918: 45)

Farjeon's deceptively simple poem takes the form of a five-act play about grief, that culminates, tragically, in the 'icy cold' of a spiritual death. Most significant, however, is the title. On one level 'The Outlet' refers to the source of comfort which fails, that is, the friend. On another it refers to the poet herself who forms the outlet for her friend's grief. Finally, though, the title is self-referential: it is the poem itself that forms the real and only outlet for her grief. Within this context both the surface conformity and the unarticulable subtext of this poetry, its 'symbolic' and its 'semiotic' inscriptions, become what Julia Kristeva has described as the 'communicable marks of an affective reality, present, palpable to the reader (I like this book because sadness – or anxiety or joy – is communicated to me by it) and nevertheless dominated, kept at a distance, vanquished' (Kristeva, 1987: 108–9). In her article 'On the melancholic imaginary' she argues that creative discourse performs a significant function within grief work:

> This literary or religious representation is not an *elaboration* in the sense of a 'becoming conscious' of the inter- and intrapsychic causes of moral pain. In this it differs from the psychoanalytic path that proposes itself for the dissolution of this symptom. However, this literary (and religious) representation possesses a real and imaginary efficacy that, cathartic more than of the order of elaboration, is a therapeutic method utilized in all societies throughout the ages.
>
> (Kristeva, 1987: 110)

If, then, poetry enables women to assume a distance from grief, it can also be seen to place them beyond the identity of 'the bereaved'. 'When the work of mourning is completed' observes Freud, 'the ego becomes free and uninhibited again' (Freud, 1917: 145). The poem frees the writer from obligations to the past, it provides an end to the search, and facilitates the formation of a new identity. Here, perhaps is the first stage of a transition from wife, to widow, to woman.

Yet there is another dimension to the grief process. Kristeva suggests that '[a]ccording to classical psychoanalytical theory . . . depression, like mourning, hides an aggression against the lost object and thereby reveals the ambivalence on the part of the afflicted with respect to the object of his mourning' (1987: 106). In the particular socio-historic context of the

First World War, what form might such an ambivalence take? If women, whose identity traditionally derives from that of their menfolk, undergo a loss of attachment to these men, then they can also be seen to be distanced from the symbolic order that would control them. In consequence, the co-existent contradictions of attachment and aggression create in mourning a double-edged phenomenon with the capacity to shift the parameters of conflict into the arena of sexual politics, a battleground thought to be safely buried by the 'higher' priority of prosecuting the war. The work of Jacqueline Rose provides a convincing demonstration of the logic that makes it impossible to divide the question of war from that of gender. Citing D. W. Winnicott's observation that '*One of the roots of the need to be a dictator can be a compulsion to deal with this fear of woman by encompassing and acting for her*', Rose links the fear of female sexuality to the desire to believe in the possibility of knowledge – of absolute truth – a concept which is central to the logic of war. Within her argument, sexuality becomes a paradigm for war's imposition of uniformity: 'unification becomes a necessary violence like, we might say, the subordination of a partial, multifarious, or even perverse sexuality to the dictates of a one-track, singular, and unified genital sex' (Rose, 1993: 35).

An awareness of the ambivalence that exists within the condition of mourning certainly puts a different perspective on one of the poems I considered earlier. Vera Brittain's 'Roundel ("Died of Wounds")', on one level symbolic of the relentless search for the lost love object, can also be seen to contain an element of resentment. 'Because you died', *because* the loved one has left her, she has been abandoned to 'brief and idle hours' beside 'lesser loves', in an empty world where 'disillusion's slow corroding stain/ will creep upon each quest but newly tried'. The love object is hated and resented for the crime of abandonment at the same time as it is cherished and mourned. This paradox is integral to the mourning process, and it also suggests why women's mourning must also possess a political dimension. In *Thoughts for the Times on War and Death*, Freud comments:

> These loved ones are on the one hand an inner possession, components of our own ego; but on the other hand they are partly strangers, even enemies. With the exception of only a very few situations, there adheres to the tenderest and most intimate of our love-relations a small portion of hostility which can excite an unconscious death-wish.
>
> (Freud, 1915: 298)

The man who is the object of Brittain's desire simultaneously represents the enemy – the patriarch who would deny her political subjectivity.[6]

The ambivalence of a hidden aggression would also seem to be present in the syntactical desperation that characterizes Violet Spender's 'The Secret'. The poem combines the memory of a lost and 'golden' past with a portrait of an unremittingly bleak present:

> And we stretch out our hands,
> Our weary hands trembling with age and toil,
> Towards the past
> Where they still are shining, . . .
> We, in our anguish, writhing here,
> Ask: "Where is God?"
> "What is God?"

(Spender, 1922: 29–30)

At this point Spender's anger seems unanswerable, her aggression seems on the verge of acknowledgement, and yet through almost inconceivable convolutions she redirects her resentment into a conventional religious posture:

> What is anything we know save a sign?
> Our very words, what are they but symbols?
> And this very love which we bear one another,
> What is it but the symbol of love still greater,
> The love of God!

(Spender, 1922: 30)

The vagueness of Spender's advocacy here seems certain above all to symbolize not the love of God, but her own uncertainty and doubts. The poem can be seen to operate within what Kristeva would describe as a 'modality of signifiance' (1987: 108), articulating as it does ideas and attitudes that cannot be directly or openly acknowledged – particularly in a society that regards the manifestation of misery as unpatriotic.

The tensions within Spender and Brittain's poems, and indeed among many of the poets examined by Khan and Montefiore, suggest another side to the loss created by the carnage of the First World War, and it seems important to ask what does the lost object (man) symbolize for these wartime women? The woman war poet, observes Jan Montefiore, 'asserts the melancholy privilege of a poetic voice predicated on the absence and – possibly – death of the loved one' (Montefiore, 1993: 62) – and, without denying the attachments that existed, the loss of the man must also be seen as the potential liberation of the woman.

Just how radical are the implications of this emergent female voice? Did the nation's patriarchs listen to the women who sought recognition? Alice Meynell's 'A Father of Women' makes a clear demand:

Figure 2 'Reverie' – A Red Cross worker.

FEMINIST REVIEW NO 51, AUTUMN 1995

Fathers of women with your honour in trust;
Approve, accept, know them daughters of men,
    Now that your sons are dust.

(Meynell, 1921: 119)

But what sort of acceptance would be implied by the transition envisaged by Meynell? An earlier stanza of the poem suggests a note of caution: 'Our father works in us,/ The daughters of his manhood' (1921: 118). Within the bounds of a rigidly patriarchal society, the daughter's progress can only be a limited one; and in a scenario which posits the daughter replacing the son as the mouthpiece of the father, the dislocations of war can be seen to encourage not change but continuity.

I do not, however, believe the picture to be quite so bleak. The ways in which women's war poetry engages with grief can give us valuable insights into the construction, fragmentation, reconstruction and displacement of female subjectivity by the ideologies of war. The expression of grief is not in itself a necessarily radical act, and identities forged in its aftermath can represent a retreat into conservative ideologies as easily as an expansion into new territory. The act of finding a voice only temporarily disassociates women from their appropriation by the patriarchal war machine and poetry as an individual response seems powerless to disturb the symbolic order, yet the writing process can be seen to symbolize the stronger new identity that Parkes has identified as a frequent outcome of the grieving process. For many women there could be no return to the deadly romantic myth of identification through their man, as the men, either temporarily or permanently, had gone. Women's war poetry is a testament to the ways in which women changed during the First World War, and to the sometimes radical, and sometimes not so radical, new identities that they formed in the fracture of war's dislocation.

There is however a coda to this picture of the interaction between war, women and creativity. At the end of the war women's poetry suddenly and mysteriously disappeared from the literary record – and this post-war disappearance gives the poetry a political cohesion that its presence could never achieve.[7] In her poem 'Women Demobilized' May Cannan describes the alienation of women in a post-war world:

Now must we go again back to the world
Full of grey ghosts and voices of men dying,
And in the rain the sounding of Last Posts,
And Lovers' crying –
Back to the old, back to the empty world.

(Cannan, 1919: 79)

This alienation was not just a personal perception – it was also political, a function of the symbolic order's need for stability in the aftermath of war's disruption. Sharon Ouditt observes that 'The war generation is not wanted by its more hard-headed, sybaritic successors: war-grief is unwelcome, reconstruction and forgetting are prioritized' (1994: 123) – perhaps a reason for the government's reluctance to institute the Armistice Day ritual of remembrance? May Cannan's autobiography emphasizes the gender specific nature of this rejection:

> The census for 1921 had found there was in the country a surplus of women who, inconsiderately had not died in the war, and now there was an outcry and someone christened them "The Surplus Two Million". *The Times* suggested they might seek work abroad; the unemployment figures were swollen with these unnecessary and unwanted persons: and the name stuck.
>
> (Cannan, 1976: 175)

Women formulate a new identity in wartime, but it would seem to be an identity that nobody wants. Single women, women without husbands, are categorized as socially useless objects by those institutions that define public opinion (the press, the pulpit and parliament). They become the 'surplus two million', a blatant acknowledgement that female subjectivity is surplus to requirements.

Grief, then, is a problem: unpatriotic in wartime and unwelcome in the brave new world of post-war reconstruction. And because the symbolic order chooses to situate it in this oppositional position, it develops the potential to become a site of resistance. I think it is possible to see grief, and the poetic monuments it erects, in opposition to and in excess of the dominant patriarchal logic of war. The poetry forms a leftover residue that resists assimilation into the history of war, and which must in consequence be repressed. Hence in the aftermath of war, these monuments, these calls to the dead, remain as semiotic irruptions within a symbolic order fundamentally unchanged by the ravages of war. In this context it is no surprise that these poems disappeared from the anthologies of war verse. They told a story that was 'other' to the official record, and as such constituted a threat. 'Paranoid impulses don't just project on to reality as delusion' observes Jacqueline Rose, 'they affect reality and become a component of it. . . . If you produce the enemy, then you must fight him' (Rose, 1993: 28–9). Real or imagined, or indeed, made real *because* so imagined, the threat was neutralized by marginalizing it. The poems were silenced because they could not be read – just as the outcry of their male authored counterparts was ultimately dismissed through their literary promotion from the voices of protest to the well-wrought urns of art. Siegfried Sassoon makes an ironic acknowledgement of this assimilation

FEMINIST REVIEW NO 51, AUTUMN 1995

when he undermines his own claims to political influence in a letter to Lady Ottoline Morrell (21 November 1917):

> But the poets will get the upper hand of them – some day (when bound in half-calf, suitable for wedding presents).
>
> (Hart-Davis, 1983: 194)

The protests of men, it would seem, are deflected through assimilation and incorporation into the very establishment whose hegemony they challenged, while women's voices can be rendered safe through the strategies of exclusion, omission and expulsion. Women's mourning was briefly recognized as a complex and subversive embodiment of anger, desire and nascent subjectivity, and in the completeness of its annihilation lies the greatest testimony to its power.

Notes

Vera Brittain's poem 'Sic Transit – (V. R., Died of Wounds, 2nd London General Hospital, Chelsea, June 9th, 1917)' and the excerpt from her poem 'Roundel', both from *Verses of a VAD* (1918) are included with the permission of Paul Berry, her literary executor.

Eleanor Farjeon's poem 'The Outlet' from *Sonnets and Poems* (Oxford University Press, 1918) is included with the permission of David Higham Associates.

The excerpt from *Siegfried Sassoon Diaries 1915–18* is reproduced by kind permission of Faber & Faber Ltd.

Every attempt has been made to contact copyright holders. The publishers would be happy to hear from any whom we have been unable to trace.

Thanks to Helen Boden and James McKinna for careful reading and emergency aid.

Gill Plain is a lecturer in English and Women's Studies at the University of Glamorgan. Her research interests include the Second World War, representations of sexuality and detective fiction. She is currently completing a book on women's fictional responses to the Second World War which will be published by Edinburgh University Press.

1 In this context it is interesting to note Julia Kristeva's observation in her article 'On the melancholic imaginary' that 'for the Catholic West, sadness is a sin and the wretched citizens of the 'abode of woe' are placed by Dante in the circles of Inferno' (Rimmon-Kenan, 1987: 105).

2 Cannadine's observation is based on comments in *The Times*, 12.11.1919.

3 Among the many 'remembrance' poems in *Scars Upon My Heart*, there are several which specifically focus on these public rituals. Examples include Dorothy

Una Ratcliffe's 'Remembrance Day in the Dales' (Reilly, 1981: 92), Eileen Newton's 'Revision' (81–2) and poems on the Cenotaph by Ursula Roberts and Charlotte Mew (93–4, 71).

4 In some of Tynan's most distressing poems, the 'common' soldier, a sinner awaiting redemption, is elevated to heroism though a mutilating salvation. The translation of physical injury into symbolic stigmata supposedly gives spiritual satisfaction to the unfortunate 'Private Flynn' (Tynan, 1916) and 'The Broken Soldier' (Tynan, 1916, reprinted in Reilly, 1981).

5 I am very grateful to Jan Montefiore for her constructive and entertaining comments and for bringing the curious opus of Violet Spender to my attention.

6 Although Sandra Gilbert's image seems rather overstated, she does make a valid point when she suggests that 'the sexual gloom expressed by so many men as well as the sexual glee experienced by so many women ultimately triggered profound feelings of guilt in a number of women' (Gilbert, 1983: 201). The guilt of the survivor is combined with grief's integral components of resentment and aggression to further complicate women's emotional and creative responses to war.

7 To reinforce this observation I undertook a brief survey of anthologies across the century. I began at the end of the war with G. H. Clarke's *A Treasury of War Poetry* (2nd ed. 1919) and Bertram Lloyd's *Poems Written During the Great War 1914–18* (1918). Of Clarke's 183 poets, 39 were clearly identifiable as women (approximately 21%), while amongst Lloyd's 29 writers, there were 5 women (17%). By 1930, women's representation had dropped to 5% in Frederick Brereton's *An Anthology of War Poems* (3 out of 60), and by the 1960s the dominant perception of war poetry had become totally synonymous with combat experience. In *Poetry of the First World War*, Maurice Hussey (1967) has one woman amongst 55 poets, while Brian Gardner's *Up the Line to Death* (1964) takes the prize for having no women at all amongst its 72 poets – in spite of boasting a section entitled 'Home Front'.

References

BOYLE, Mary E. (1916) *Aftermath* Cambridge: Heffer.

BRERETON, Frederic (1930) editor, *An Anthology of War Poems* London: Collins.

BRITTAIN, Vera (1933/78) *Testament of Youth* London: Virago.

—— (1918/95) *Verses of a VAD* London: Imperial War Museum (forthcoming).

—— (1934) *Poems of the War and After* London: Victor Gollancz.

CANNADINE, David (1981) 'War and death, grief and mourning in modern Britain' in **Whaley** (1981).

CANNAN, May Wedderburn (1919) *The Splendid Days* Oxford: Blackwell.

—— (1976) *Grey Ghosts and Voices* Kineton: The Roundwood Press.

CLARKE, George Herbert (1919) editor, *A Treasury of War Poetry* London: Hodder & Stoughton.

FARJEON, Eleanor (1918) *Sonnets and Poems* Oxford: Blackwell.

FREUD, Sigmund (1915) 'Thoughts for the times on war and death', in **Freud** (1978).

—— (1917) 'Mourning and melancholia', in **Freud** (1978).

—— (1978) *The Standard Edition of the Complete Psychological Works* Vol. XIV, edited by James Strachey, London: Hogarth.

GARDNER, Brian (1964) editor, *Up the Line to Death* London: Methuen.

GILBERT, Sandra (1983) 'Soldier's heart: literary men, literary women, and the Great War', in **Higonnet, Jenson, Michel** and **Weitz** (1987).

GOLDMAN, Dorothy (1993) *Women and World War I: The Written Response* Basingstoke: Macmillan.

HART-DAVIS, Rupert (1983) editor, *Siegfried Sassoon Diaries 1915–1918* London: Faber & Faber.

HIGONNET, Margaret Randolph, JENSON, Jane, MICHEL, Sonya and WEITZ, Margaret Collins (1987) editors, *Behind the Lines: Gender and the Two World Wars* New Haven: Yale University Press.

HUSSEY, Maurice (1967) editor, *Poetry of the First World War* London: Longman.

JONES, Peter (1972) *Imagist Poetry* Harmondsworth: Penguin.

KAHN, Nosheen (1989) *Women's Poetry of the First World War* Brighton: Harvester.

KRISTEVA, Julia (1974) 'Revolution in poetic language', in **Moi** (1986).

—— (1987) 'On the melancholic imaginary', in **Rimmon-Kenan** (1987).

LLOYD, Bertram (1918) editor, *Poems Written During the Great War* London: George Allen & Unwin.

MEYNELL, Alice (1921) *Poems* enlarged edition, London: Burns, Oates & Washbourne.

MOI, Toril (1986) editor, *The Kristeva Reader* Oxford: Blackwell.

MONTEFIORE, Jan (1993) '"Shining Pins and Wailing Shells": women poets and the Great War', in **Goldman** (1993).

OUDITT, Sharon (1994) *Fighting Forces, Writing Women* London: Routledge.

PARKES, Colin Murray (1972/86) *Bereavement* Harmondsworth: Penguin.

REILLY, Catherine (1981) *Scars Upon My Heart* London: Virago.

RIMMON-KENAN, Schlomith (1987) editor, *Discourse in Psychoanalysis and Literature* London: Methuen.

ROSE, Jacqueline (1993) *Why War?* Oxford: Blackwell.

SCHWEIK, Susan (1987) 'Writing war poetry like a woman', in **Showalter** (1989).

SHOWALTER, Elaine (1989) editor, *Speaking of Gender* London: Routledge.

SPENDER, Violet (1922) *The Path to Caister and Other Poems* London: Sidgwick & Jackson.

STONE, Gilbert (1917) editor, *Women War Workers* London: Harrap.

TAYLOR, A. J. P. (1965/92) *English History 1914–1945* Oxford: Oxford University Press.

THOMPSON, Theodora (1918) *The Coming Dawn* London: John Lane.

TYLEE, Clare (1990) *The Great War and Women's Consciousness* Basingstoke: Macmillan.

TYNAN, Katharine (1916) *The Holy War* London: Sidgwick & Jackson.

WHALEY, Joachim (1981) editor, *Mirrors of Mortality: Studies in the Social History of Death* London: Europa.

WINTER, J. M. (1981) *The Great War and the British People* Basingstoke: Macmillan.

Poem

Evlynn Sharp

FEMINIST REVIEW NO 51, AUTUMN 1995, pp. 66–67

for my grandmother, Rose

the woman emigrant

I
Before the last breath
a name rises from your voice,
brushing across the pillow
like a soft breeze,
and there is passion on your lips
remembering home.
A young woman
passes you a tumbler full of water,
she says, *do you know me now*,
as you drain the glass.
Outside on the balcony,
shadows sweep, the sky
returns to silver, and you
ask, *how far will I walk tonight?*

II
The woman runs her warm fingers through my hair,
a moment is connecting us, a dark cork falls out of air.

III
Bowls cool down the broth we share, afraid
to drink because we might rinse away
our ancestors easing out beneath the tongue.

In the yard, a new tap is being built
but an elder goes to wash herself the old way,
at the far side of the field, and nature shows
her once more the nearest drifting shallow.
Even a fish re-appearing on the river's bed
receives something constant, like water.

IV
Artificial lights glare through the pane.

Your breath is on my shoulder.
I turn around and you look older.

You shield my eyes.

Real rain beats underneath the tree opposite.
Love was growing here.
You swing a kettle.
All matter is relevant
in a country whose name
follows me, into the darkness.

Creating a Space for Absent Voices:

Disabled Women's Experience of Receiving Assistance with Daily Living Activities

Jenny Morris

FEMINIST REVIEW NO 51, AUTUMN 1995, pp. 68–93

Abstract

Feminist research on community care and 'informal carers' identified this as a women's issue but failed to address the interests and experiences of older and disabled women – those who received 'care'. One consequence is that such feminist research has implicitly, and sometimes explicitly, undermined disabled women's rights to a home, children and personal relationships. Using qualitative research, the article highlights the actual experience of women whose physical impairment means that they need help with daily living activities, looking at the different circumstances in which such help is received.

The disability movement's concept of 'independent living' raises particular issues for disabled women. 'Independent living' is about having choice and control over the assistance needed, rather than necessarily doing everything for yourself. However, gender inequalities may also inhibit the choice and control that women have in their lives.

Assistance can be given within a personal relationship as an expression of love, but disabled women may also experience abusive, restrictive or exploitative relationships. Public services do not generally provide assistance in a way which enables a woman to have choice and control in her life, or even to carry out child-caring or homemaking tasks. The research on the various ways of receiving personal assistance found that those women who were able to purchase their own help were most likely to be living independently, in the sense of exerting choice and control in their lives.

Feminist research can help to create a space for disabled women's absent voices, and add to the pressure for change in the way that personal assistance needs are met. This is a human and civil rights issue which has a key impact on the control that disabled women have over their lives.

Keywords

Disabled women; feminist research; community care; independent living; qualitative research; disability

Introduction

Qualitative research has always had a special role in feminist sociology. In-depth interviews are more effective in both reaching an understanding of the reality of women's daily lives and in creating a space for women's voices to be heard. But for disabled people qualitative research has a particularly important role to play in furthering our civil and human rights.

All forms of prejudice have at their heart a refusal to identify with a person's reality, setting them apart from common humanity. This is a very important part of the prejudice experienced by disabled people, based as it often is on an assumption that the quality of our lives is so poor that they are not worth living – and therefore an unwillingness to identify with our reality. Unfortunately, the way that some feminist sociologists have excluded disabled women's subjective reality from their qualitative research has colluded with these prejudicial assumptions.

Dorothy Smith says that feminist research is characterized by a method which, 'at the outset of inquiry, creates the space for an absent subject, and an absent experience, that is to be filled with the presence and spoken experience of actual women speaking of and in the actualities of their everyday worlds' (Smith, 1988: 107). The research on which this article is based was an attempt to 'create the space for an absent subject' – in this instance, the experiences of those men and women whose level of physical impairment meant that they required help with the tasks of daily living. It is published in a number of forms (see Morris, 1993a and 1993b) but the purpose of this article is to create a space for the voices of disabled *women* to be heard and, in so doing, to examine whether community care policies have particular implications for women who need physical help in order to go about their daily lives.

I start by looking at feminist research on 'informal carers' (that is, those family members, neighbours or friends who give unpaid assistance to people who experience physical, sensory or intellectual impairment, or emotional distress) summarizing some of the analysis which I have developed in more detail elsewhere (Morris, 1991: Chapter 6; Morris, 1993b: Chapter 3). Feminist research in this area articulated important criticisms of community care policies but, while such policies were unfolding during the 1980s, the disability movement was developing its own attack, based on the concept of independent living. The next section of the article therefore looks at the challenge mounted to notions of 'care' and 'caring' by the disability movement and at the particular implications that the concept of independent living has for disabled women.

69

The main body of the article is, however, concerned with an account of what it is like for disabled women to receive physical help within personal relationships, from statutory services, and from paid employees. Disabled women's experience of providing emotional and physical support themselves within personal relationships is also explored. These experiences raise important social policy issues – which have been almost entirely missing from (or else contradicted by) the feminist agenda on 'caring'. The final part of the article identifies what these social policy issues are, arguing that the feminist perspective on community care must incorporate the concerns of the disability movement.

Silencing our voices

Feminist research during the 1980s stressed that the unpaid caring work which women carry out for children and for family members who are old and/or disabled is an important part of women's experience of oppression. This research was particularly addressed to the development, during the same decade, of government policies aimed at reducing the numbers of people in various forms of institutional care, increasing the opportunities for disabled and older people to live in (or remain living in) 'ordinary' homes in the community. These policies, which were finally implemented in the 1990 NHS and Community Care Act, were undoubtedly primarily motivated by the tenfold increase between 1978 and 1986 in the social security budget being spent on residential care for older people. While social services departments – as the main agency involved in implementing the 1990 Act – have been exhorted by government guidance to see living in the 'community', rather than residential care, as the preferred option for older and disabled people, feminist research has constantly reminded both policy-makers and social services practitioners that all too often it is women's unpaid work of looking after disabled and older family members which makes such an option possible.

During the 1980s, this unpaid work has become more recognized by policy-makers and by health and social services professionals – partly because it *has* to be recognized in order for community care to succeed as a policy. However, the identification of 'informal carers' as a social group was also firmly placed on the social policy agenda by the growth of the Carers' National Association and by the increasing body of research on the experience of 'caring'. The foundations for this research were laid down by a paper presented by Janet Finch and Dulcie Groves in 1979 which cut through 'the euphemistic language of "community" and "family" to argue that community care was essentially about the care provided by women; and it discussed the effects of caring on women's life chances in terms of equality of opportunities with men' (Baldwin and Twigg, 1991: 118).

© Angela Martin

There followed a decade of research and theorizing about 'care' and 'caring', dominated by a feminist agenda of challenging the economic dependence of women created by their role of unpaid carers within the family.

This agenda constructed older and disabled people as 'dependent people', focusing on 'the burden of care' which was imposed on women within the family. Such an agenda excluded the subjective experience of older and disabled people. As both Lois Keith (1992) and myself (1991: Chapter 6) have pointed out, feminist researchers on 'informal care' concentrated almost solely on the experience of those women they called 'carers', constructing an analysis which allowed no room for the subjective reality of those who are 'cared for'. This research therefore colluded with prejudicial social attitudes which are commonly held about older and disabled people – at the core of which is the failure to identify with such experiences.

Feminist research on community care identified the area as a 'women's issue' but generally failed to incorporate old or disabled women into the category of 'women'. One result of this has been the ability of some feminists to feel that a denial of a home and family life – i.e., consignment to residential care – are appropriate policy reactions to the needs associated with growing older or experiencing physical, sensory or intellectual impairment (see Morris, 1991: Chapter 6 and Morris, 1993b: Chapter 3 for a detailed critique of feminist research on informal care). Dalley, for example, has argued that the 'bed-bound' young mother could develop an 'ungendered' role if she lived in a group house (Dalley, 1988: 122). And Finch claims that taking disabled people out of their own homes and providing the help they need in 'a range of residential facilities' is to be supported because it would de-emphasize 'family care as the central feature of community care'. She goes on to say that this

> might well receive the support of handicapped people [sic] themselves, for whom personal independence is a key goal. . . . Of course within such settings attention would need to be paid to enabling people to maintain links with people (relatives or friends) to whom they are emotionally close, that is, people who care 'about' them; but in my view, removing the compulsion to perform the labour of caring 'for' one's relatives is likely to facilitate rather than to obstruct that.
>
> (Finch, 1990: 55)

Such patronising, cavalier, *discriminatory* attitudes towards disabled people are only possible because feminists such as Finch and Dalley do not identify with our subjective reality. Our rights to have a home of our own, to live with those we love and who love us, our rights to have children and to bring them up in the way that nondisabled women take for granted, are not even considered in the debate about the sexual division of the labour of caring within heterosexual family households.

The denial of the opportunity to create a home, bear and rear children, to care generally for others, has particular implications for disabled women and this is discussed later in this article.

In the last few years the perspective on women's caring role which dominated feminist research in the 1980s has started to be re-examined in the light of a recognition that some groups of women experience a denial of the opportunity to care for children and other family members and that this may also be part of an experience of oppression. Hilary Graham, for example, has reassessed her earlier analysis of the concept of caring (Graham, 1983) and argues that, while the feminist research on caring in the 1980s was actually about white, middle-class women's experience, Black, working-class women are often denied the opportunity of caring for family members. 'Thus, rather than experienced in oppressive ways, caring for partners, children and older relatives can be experienced as a way of resisting racial and class oppression' (Graham, 1991: 69). Jan Walmsley, in looking at the lives of women with learning difficulties, argues that 'For some women who are denied the opportunity to be carers caring becomes a valued activity to be sought, rather than an oppressive burden to be shifted' (Walmsley, 1993: 131).

There has also been increasing criticism in recent years of the way that feminist research, purporting to be giving voice to women's experiences, has been from the point of view of nondisabled women (Keith, 1992; Morris, 1991). In *Pride Against Prejudice* (1991) I argued that a failure to consider the point of view of those who receive 'care' means that research and analysis on the experience of caring is very incomplete. Research which concerned this experience may well challenge the assumption that, within families, there is a straightforward division between those who are carers and those who are cared for.

> If we focused not just on the subjective experience of those identified as carers but also on the other party to the caring relationship we may find that in some situations the roles are blurred or shifting. We may also want to expand our definition of caring to encompass not just physical tasks but also the emotional part of caring for relationships. Research carried out by disabled feminists would therefore focus not so much on *carers* as on *caring*.
>
> (Morris, 1991: 167)

This article is a partial attempt to take up my own challenge. While motivated by a feminist perspective it is also framed by the concerns of the disabled people's movement and, in particular, by the concept of independent living as it has been developed by that movement. I therefore want to now look at how the disability movement has challenged the concepts of 'care' and 'caring' by the re-examination of the meanings of 'dependence' and 'independence', before moving on to identify that this challenge raises particular issues for disabled women, issues which reveal significant limitations to the feminist research on caring.

Challenging concepts of dependence and independence

The meanings of the words 'dependence' and 'independence' have been re-examined and re-defined by many disabled individuals and disability organizations since the 1970s. There is a strong sense among such people of belonging to an international independent living movement which had its origins in Berkeley, California but which now has a presence in many other developed and developing countries. This was reflected in the worldwide representation of disabled people at the international congress 'Independence 92'.

Unfortunately, the term 'independent living' has, during the 1980s and early 1990s, sometimes been used by health or social services professionals to describe initiatives which they have developed in the context of community care policies. Focusing on professional assessments of functional ability and inability, these initiatives often bear little relationship to the principles and practice of the independent living movement. It is therefore important to set out clearly the philosophy and practice of that movement.

The philosophy of the independent living movement is based on four assumptions:

– that all human life is of value;
– that anyone, whatever their impairment, is capable of exerting choices;
– that people who are disabled by society's reaction to physical, intellectual and sensory impairment and to emotional distress have the right to assert control over their lives;
– that disabled people have the right fully to participate in society.

The concept of independent living is a broad one, embracing as it does the full range of human and civil rights. This means the right to have personal relationships, to be a parent, the right to equal access to education, training, employment and leisure activities and the right to participate in the life of the community. The movement is clear that its aims and aspirations are as relevant to those with intellectual impairments, to older people (including those with conditions such as Alzheimer's Disease), and to those who are survivors of the mental health system, as they are to the stereotype of the fit, young male paraplegic.

In developing the philosophy of independent living, disabled people have had to redefine the meaning of the word 'independent' (see Oliver, 1991: 91). In Western industrial societies, this term has commonly been associated with the ability to do things for oneself, to be self-supporting, self-reliant. When physical impairment means that there are things that someone cannot do for themselves, daily living tasks which they need help with, the assumption is that this person is 'dependent'. And in Western culture to be dependent is to be subordinate, to be subject to the control of others. Much of the literature on community care refers to 'dependent people', most rehabilitation services focus on the 'independence' which is to be gained by maximizing physical mobility and physical ability to do daily living tasks. Those who cannot do things for themselves are assumed to be unable to control their lives.

In the context of the economic inequality which accompanies significant physical impairment in industrialized societies (and this is particularly the case for women), the need for personal assistance has been translated into a need for 'care' in the sense of a need to be looked after. Once personal assistance is seen as 'care' then the 'carer', whether a paid worker or an unpaid relative or friend, becomes the person in charge, the person in control. The disabled person is seen as being dependent on the carer, and incapable even of taking charge of the personal assistance s/he requires (see

Mason, 1992: 80).

The independent living movement challenges all this. Simon Brisenden pointed out that disabled people experience:

> an ideology of independence. It teaches us that unless we can do everything for ourselves we cannot take our place in society. We must be able to cook, wash, dress ourselves, make the bed, write, speak and so forth, before we can become proper people, before we are 'independent'.

(Brisenden, 1989: 9)

Brisenden goes on to say that the independent living movement, in contrast, uses the word 'independent'

> in a practical and commonsense way to mean simply being able to achieve our goals. The point is that independent people have control over their lives, not that they perform every task themselves. Independence is not linked to the physical or intellectual capacity to care for oneself without assistance; independence is created by having assistance when and how one requires it.

(1989: 9)

Control over the assistance that is required to go about daily life is crucial, therefore, to the concept of independent living. It is this control which enables the expression of individuality and from this then flows the assertion of disabled people's human rights and their status as citizens. Control over personal assistance is necessary if those who need help with physical tasks are to achieve both human and civil rights, in other words not only the right to have control over basic daily living tasks (such as when to get up, go to bed, go to the toilet, when and what to eat) but also the right to have personal and sexual relationships, to seek employment, to engage in leisure and political activities.

Disabled women, independence and independent living

The concept of independent living raises particular concerns for disabled women in that their experience of oppression as a result of their gender may also reduce opportunities for independence. Many nondisabled women experience a lack of control over their lives because of their lack of economic independence and the way that sexism curtails their autonomy.

Disabled women who have personal assistance requirements and who are economically dependent within a heterosexual family context – as wife, mother or daughter – will have particular difficulty in asserting their autonomy. Such difficulties are compounded by sexist assumptions that undermine nondisabled and disabled women's ability to act independently or indeed to consider themselves as autonomous human beings. However, while feminist analysis has traditionally located the creation of women's dependency in the sexual division of labour within the family and in the social construction of masculinity and femininity, such an analysis does not satisfactorily represent disabled women's experience of oppression.

Disabled women's aspirations for independent living – in the sense of being able fully to participate in society – are to a large extent similar to those of disabled men. However, many women who are disabled by society's reaction to their impairment experience the obstacles placed in the way of their fulfilling what it is to be a woman in our society to be a crucial part of their oppression. For example, earlier research with which I was involved – a collective project carried out by women paralysed by spinal cord injury and published as *Able Lives: Women's Experience of Paralysis* – illustrated the way in which many newly paralysed women measured their lives by the extent to which they were able to fulfil their roles as wives and mothers.

> As women, part of our return to 'normal' life is often a return to the pressures of looking after other people. Aids and adaptations which are supposedly about helping us to be [physically] independent are in fact often about enabling others to be dependent on us for the tasks which keep a house clean and a family fed. Society's expectations of women being what they are, it is not surprising that many of us measure our 'success' or 'failure' in terms of whether we can return to the role of housewife and mother.
>
> (Morris, 1989: 52)

It is very important, however, to resist the tendency to present such a goal as motivated by some kind of false consciousness, to assume that disabled women striving to be wives and mothers are merely victims of sexist ideology. Having sexual relationships (whether they are heterosexual or lesbian relationships), family relationships, bearing and rearing children, making a home – all these are important human and civil rights which, if denied to *non*disabled women, would be the subject of outrage.

The majority of nondisabled heterosexual feminists do not abandon relationships with men, do not reject motherhood, do not reject family relationships nor the desire to have a comfortable home life. Yet in the name of resisting the sexual division of labour, disabled women have been invited to be pioneers in some kind of brave new world of residential establishments. This, as we have seen, has been the prescription of feminists such as Janet Finch and Gillian Dalley when they addressed the sexual division of labour within the family when it comes to providing assistance for its older and disabled members.

I want to now look at some of the situations in which women experience physical help with daily living activities, identifying some factors which can influence women's experience of independence and dependence, but above all giving expression to a subjective reality which has been generally excluded from feminist analysis. The interview material contained in the next section of this article comes from research carried out in 1992. Fifty people were interviewed who lived in one of four different parts of England, which included north and south, inner city, town and rural areas. Ages ranged from 19 to 55 and there was a wide experience represented in terms of educational background, employment status and income. Contacts were made through social services area teams, independent living projects, organizations of and organizations for disabled people. The sample covered a wide range of situations and physical impairments (including those with significant speech impairments), the common factor being that people required at least some personal assistance in their daily lives. Additional sampling was carried out to ensure that Black and ethnic minority people and gay men and lesbians were properly represented.

While the full analysis of the interviews (see Morris, 1993b) focuses on the experience of men and women who received personal assistance in the context of residential care, within personal relationships, from domiciliary services and from paid employees, this article concentrates on the experiences of disabled women who received help in a variety of forms within their own home. This is the experience which is missing from the feminist research on caring and which needs to be incorporated into any feminist analysis of community care.

Receiving help within personal relationships

Apart from residential care, there are three sources of help with daily living tasks: the people with whom someone has personal relationships – partners, parents, siblings, children, friends; statutory services; and those employed by the person requiring help. For many, family members are the first and often the only source of help.

Love, intimacy, dependence and independence

For some women, receiving help within a personal relationship is an expression of love. This was Moira's experience when, as a child and adolescent, she received help from her mother.

> I was terrible when I was a teenager and in a funny way I think that the physical help I got from Mum was like a piece of calm in the middle of all that turmoil. I mean, we could be having the most awful row and yet when she helped me onto the loo it would all go quiet. Maybe it was that she'd done it all those years with . . . you know . . . well, love I suppose . . . so doing those physical things was associated with good things for us. And she was the best at doing it, the next best thing to doing it myself, well it *was* like doing it myself. Because she cared as much as I would about doing it right.

Sometimes the intimacy of a loving relationship can seem the most appropriate context for help with personal care. Jackie said:

> I think if you have a relationship with someone you do have a basic recognition of someone as a human being and that makes it allright. . . . Also, there's a lot of trust there, a lot of knowledge and trust . . . I think there's an absence of embarrassment, you know if you need help in the loo or the bath or around bed-time, you're not likely to be embarrassed with your partner. There's intimacy.

However, some people, particularly those who as adults receive personal assistance from a parent, are made to feel dependent by the context in which the help is provided. A parent's natural wish to protect and look after his/her child can become an inhibiting restraint especially when the world outside the home provides little opportunity for independence. Young disabled women, in particular, may find that both their family and society act in ways which increase dependence rather than encouraging independence.

Some young disabled women interviewed found that no other role is open to them than that of a dependent child. Rosemary, for example, found that her parents continued to be very protective towards her and discouraged her from having a life outside her home as she grew up.

> Where we lived at the time was very isolated and there was no way I could at the time . . . I couldn't actually get out. I don't think my mother was really interested in me doing that anyway. The trouble is my sister is eight years older than me. There's quite a generation gap and when she left home . . . when she became independent perhaps things were different. She got married about twenty and left home and I was left as the baby. I suppose I was quite shy and it's very difficult because people don't always take you for your age, they sort of ask you what school you go to.

Rosemary has gradually been able to assert her need for a home of her own and for the physical assistance she needs to be provided outside of a family context. This has partly occurred because, as her parents grow older, they have become more reliant on Rosemary herself for assistance. Such reciprocity has both created a more equal relationship and also given Rosemary the added incentive of realizing that she will soon have to manage without her parents' help anyway.

Rosemary's move in the next few months into a housing association property comes when she is in her late thirties. Other women interviewed found that their only prospect of moving away from the parental home was to move into residential care. This was Laura's 'choice' and provoked much conflict within her family as her benefits were an important part of the household income.

Difficult though it is for a young disabled person, particularly a young woman, to assert independence from his/her parents, the issues are yet clearer for an adult asserting independence from a parent than they are for women asserting independence within heterosexual couple relationships.

Catherine lives with Robert and she talked of the tension between valuing the intimacy of the personal assistance that he gives her and the independence that she gains from receiving help from a paid helper. Robert has always found it difficult having someone else helping Catherine:

> Sometimes I picked up from him that he was being quite protective and if he saw somebody . . . a couple of times I've had helpers who haven't been very good at lifting and things like that and if he saw that going on then he'd get quite protective. But I don't think that was the overriding thing. . . . I think he thought he was the best, yes. I think he certainly had that. And that was important to him. I think it was important to me too.

When their relationship broke down Catherine discovered advantages to employing someone to help her get up in the morning and go to bed at night in that it gave her greater freedom and reliability. 'Another thing I've quite enjoyed', she said, 'is having another woman to help and do things like putting earrings in – which freaks Robert out – or trying my hair in a different way . . . there are just some things he just can't do.'

When they got back together again, Catherine found that while she wanted to continue to have at least some paid help in the mornings:

> He's quite reluctant to have a lot of input from someone else. It's quite flattering really – he's very pleased to be doing the helping again . . . he's proud that he knows what to do and can do it. I have to watch myself, I have to let him know that others can do it as well. . . . We're trying to work all these things out at the moment. We've discussed about me needing help and about me enjoying more freedom when he wasn't around and what to do about that. We haven't come to a conclusion yet together but I'm thinking of asking the Council to pay for help three times a week, say Tuesdays to Thursdays so that we have the long weekends totally on our own. . . . The trouble with having people coming in is that we are at our most intimate last thing at night and first thing in the morning.

Balancing the need for privacy and intimacy within personal relationships with the advantages of receiving outside help is a common experience of both men and women who require help with daily living activities. However, for women living in heterosexual couple relationships there will often be particular difficulties associated with an assertion of independence.

Protecting loving relationships
Another part of the complex relationship between independence and dependency within personal relationships is made clear by the way in

which many people interviewed identified that getting help from sources outside family and personal relationships was vital to protecting these relationships.

Women who need help with daily living tasks struggle to participate in equal relationships with friends, partners, parents, children. Many of the women (and men) interviewed spoke of the balance which needed to be struck in their lives between choosing to receive intimate personal assistance from someone they loved, and who loved them, and yet trying to get access to alternative sources of assistance which were necessary in order to protect their relationship. This struggle was summed up by Jackie, who is parenting within a lesbian relationship:

> With the personal assistance I get within my relationship, I think you have to be careful, there is a danger of becoming over-dependent and overly tied to each other and just not having any space and losing respect and losing interest in each other. And of the relationship potentially becoming quite abusive in both directions. If someone's over-tired and has been doing too much of the looking-after of you they can get pretty pissed off and have a go at you. And equally, if you're close to someone and they're doing a lot of things for you and they're doing them over and over again, it's easy for you to forget that they're a person.

> If there's quite a good balance in my life in terms of getting support and being able to do things in different ways and in different environments and stuff then it's really lovely to have Ros doing things for me because it's part of a loving relationship. But when it goes out of balance and it seems to be only Ros, it's absolutely dreadful and you lose sight of the fact that we're lovers and that we're individuals and that we do actually love each other, because there's no space for it left.

While many people felt that the help they received from family members or a partner was 'the best', it was also clear that assistance received from those who were paid to give it was often necessary to supplement this help. For example, although Julie wanted to receive assistance from those she loved, it was important to her that she also received help from people who were paid to give that help.

> For intimate personal care I prefer my sister or David to anybody else but if it's for any other sort of care I would prefer social services because I'm more in control, more directing things.

She was also acutely aware of the way that having to rely on friends could disturb the balance of a friendship.

> I really dislike having to call on friends for anything really . . . I mean it doesn't matter how often they say they don't mind it, I just resent the fact that I have to ask for it anyway. So I would always prefer somebody that's being paid for it, whether it's being paid for directly by me or by social services.

Powerlessness and abuse

Most of the women interviewed were aware of the importance of reciprocity within personal relationships if dependence on someone for physical help was not to create an unequal relationship. They were also aware of the importance of other sources of help in protecting their personal relationships. Some women, however, experienced relationships characterized by powerlessness and an inability to gain support from outside the home and for some this was associated with serious physical, emotional and/or sexual abuse.

Not one of the people whom I interviewed who had experienced, or were currently experiencing abuse had felt able to disclose this to any of the health or social service professionals with whom they were in contact. A number of them had, however, tried to escape the abusive situation by trying to get their local housing authority to respond to their wish to be rehoused. Paula, for example, who had been physically and sexually abused by her father for as long as she could remember, applied to her local council to be rehoused in her late teens. 'But they said, you know, they had done all this work to my parents' flat . . . put in a ramp and that.' She went on:

> I can't talk about IT . . . you know, capital letters IT and all that . . . I know I should but there it is . . . What I can tell you is how I got away, escaped . . . I used to go to a day centre and we had a talk from a woman with a disability herself . . . it was about welfare rights or something . . . anyway, I got to know her and she told me about the ILF [Independent Living Fund] and she also put me in touch with the housing association which owns this place and so there we are, I made it. I'm very lucky really.

The local housing authority's failure to respond to Paula's expression of her need for independent housing meant that she could not escape an abusive situation for many years. Disabled women living with violent husbands may also have similar difficulties in getting their housing need recognized. As Audrey said:

> I wanted to leave for a long time but where can you go when you've got a specially built place which can accommodate a wheelchair and the council says you're housed? And where do you go when you've got young children and there's nowhere to go that's accessible?

By the time Audrey's neighbours contacted social services on her behalf because of her husband's behaviour, Audrey's sons were in their teens and she accepted the one bedroom flat which was the only alternative housing on offer. She said, 'I wanted to get away completely, I felt I had done my bit as a mother. I wanted to get away because my husband was making them a bit like he was.'

For any disabled person experiencing abuse there will be particular difficulties in disclosing the abuse when the abuser is also the person on whom they rely for the practical assistance which makes daily survival possible. These difficulties are only compounded by a failure of statutory organizations to recognize disabled people's aspirations for independent housing and assistance.

The experience of statutory services

It was clear from the experience of those women interviewed that a reliance on services (provided by social services and health authorities) did not generally enable women to participate in personal relationships or engage in work or social activities outside their home in a way which they would choose.

There was a particularly common failure of statutory services to respond to the personal assistance needs that women had related to their roles as carers within their household. This has been encouraged by the tendency of home *help* services in recent years to turn themselves into home *care* services, focusing on personal care (see, for example, RADAR and Arthritis Care, 1991). This means that not only is it now more difficult to get help with housework but it is particularly difficult to get help with looking after children or anything else which is not deemed to be personal care (i.e., getting up, getting dressed, bathing, going to the toilet, eating).

Moira, for example, found that when her daughter was born her social services department said that their home carers would not be able to help her care for the baby. 'It wasn't in their job description and they suggested that my mother helped me.' This was an important motivation in her application for a cash grant from her social services department to enable her to employ her own helpers who make it possible for her to look after her daughter.

Jackie found that, when she became unable to do the kind of things which she normally did as part of her contribution to running the household, the only help she could get from the social services department was with personal care.

> The thing that they didn't recognize at all . . . they didn't accept that there were things that I did in the household [and that] therefore part of what the carers [from social services] should do should be the things that I would have done. Like the shopping, putting Dan's washing on and, I don't know, we worked out a great long list of domestic things that I normally did.

To women who see their role within their household as that of the homemaker and child-carer, the inability to get the help they need to

© Angela Martin

continue this role is a particularly oppressive experience. Disabled women are commonly represented as passive recipients of care yet the role of care-giver is an important one to many of them.

Outside the home and family life, there are few roles open to disabled women. Only 31 per cent of disabled women of working age are in paid employment (OPCS, 1988). Statutory services add to the pressures on women to be confined within their own home by failing to offer any help with going outside the home, or even help to leave the home. For example, while Bina's social services department provides her with help within her home, they will not help her with getting in and out of her car. And Elizabeth, who relies on the Meals-on-Wheels service, found that, once she got a part-time job the service could not respond to her needs. 'I wanted them to bring it to my workplace, which is only just across the road, but they said it wasn't on their route'. Elizabeth's request for a service to be delivered to her workplace was not compatible with the assumption that Meals-on-Wheels deliver a service to people in their own homes.

Valerie summed up the experience many women had of statutory services when she said:

> I think the community care philosophy doesn't understand what independent living is. . . . They seem to think that community care is about someone being cosy and comfortable, being kept clean. To me that's a step back into the

84

situation of residential care – living in the contained environment of your own home.

A further barrier to disabled women exerting control over their lives is that statutory services tend to be delivered in ways which make it difficult for disabled women to assert their own perceptions of what they need. Elizabeth described how her local authority Family Aides are 'very patronizing. . . . They're overbearing. . . . They want to give help in a custodial sense rather than facilitate. It's a big difference. When you're being custodial you're . . . well you're dictating aren't you, more or less, you're smothering a person's sense of independence'. She spoke eloquently of how the service providers' philosophy doesn't fit in with what she perceives her needs to be.

> For example, I had a confrontation with them when I returned from university last summer. I put it to them that when I got a job I would get more exhausted and I would want to have help in ways which I hadn't had before . . . like feeding. Because when I'm tired my athetoid movements [which mean that her body shakes] become more uncontrollable and obviously feeding myself becomes even more of an effort. So I just said, 'would you help me, say, on the day I had an interview and I wanted to conserve all my energy?' One of them said that was like regressing. They more or less implied that when I was at university and got support from Community Service Volunteers (CSVs) that I had become lazy. They were trying to make out that I was sort of trying to put one over.

Disabled women often try to assert their independence, in the sense of taking control over the help that they need to go about their daily lives, only to be confronted by the assumption commonly held by professionals and care workers that *they* have the right to define what is needed and how help should be given. This creates a real barrier to disabled women's participation in both personal relationships and the wider society generally. Particular difficulties are created by the common failure to recognize disabled women's caring role and this is discussed in more detail later.

Purchasing personal assistance

Some women who require practical assistance with daily living activities are able to employ helpers, using cash grants from the Independent Living Fund and/or their social services authority or their own resources. Having this kind of control over how help is provided enables women to participate both in personal relationships and in the wider society. For example, Lauren, who requires 24-hour help, employs four workers on a shift system using a cash grant from her social services authority. Now in her fifties, she has brought up her son on her own, works full time and looks after her 80-year-old mother.

Maria, now in her forties, described the contrast between her experience of having to rely on her boyfriend for help when she was first disabled and her current experience of independence.

> Basically it broke up my relationship because the guy I was living with was doing all those caring jobs which he shouldn't have had to have done . . . not that he ever objected to doing it but it changed the nature of our relationship totally. I think had I been secure with having someone to deal with all my day-to-day care there would have been room for us to have our relationship.

Now, she employs two people (one working from Monday to Friday, the other at the week-ends) to help her.

> It means I can get up in the morning when I want to, go to bed in the evening when I want to, go out when I want to, and lead the kind of life that I want to. . . . To not be reliant on my family and my friends . . . to keep all that separate [so that] to them I'm me rather than someone who needs help.

Catherine described the advantages of having a paid helper instead of having to rely totally on her partner.

> It's very difficult to ask somebody that you're also in a loving relationship with, it's very difficult to constantly ask them for the basic things you need. I find it's a sort of breath of fresh air in a way when my helper comes in and I have loads and loads and different things that I couldn't ask Robert to do. They're different things each time, there aren't certain things that I don't ask him to do, but if something was really annoying me, I don't know, a mark on the window, something like that. Sometimes I might ask him to do that, but other times I save those things up until the helper comes so that I could ask them. I know that there'll be no strings, no other strings attached to asking, it's just a straight can you do that.

Having the resources to pay for the kind of help that a disabled woman wants, when she wants it, in the way that she chooses, enables a woman to play an equal part in the household in which she lives and in personal relationships. The control which comes from purchasing assistance, rather than relying on statutory services where service deliverers determine the nature of the help given, can be crucial to a woman's feelings about herself. Moira, for example, described how being able to specify exactly what and how help should be given, promotes her self-esteem.

> If I'm going somewhere special and I want to make sure I look good, I need someone to take a great deal of trouble with arranging my clothes, putting my make-up on, doing my hair. They need to be patient and I'm paying for that patience so I feel OK about expecting it. I can't imagine someone employed by social services ever following my instructions in that way, they've got someone else giving them instructions. It wasn't until I employed my own helpers that I could afford to think about what I looked like, what I wanted to look like

because even if I had cared about what I looked like I couldn't have done anything about it.

Elizabeth, who currently relies on statutory services, wishes that she could have more control over the help that she gets. 'Ideally I should be able to have a helper who can do my hair. I'm not being racist but white people generally don't know how to look after Afro hair.' If she were able to employ helpers in the way that Moira does she would choose to recruit someone who had the skills she requires.

These various experiences of receiving help with daily living tasks – from family and friends, statutory services and paid helpers – challenge some of the assumptions commonly made by feminist research on community care. Two particular points need to be stressed:

- Physical impairment – the functional limitations which restrict what people can do for themselves – does not in itself create dependency. Rather it is the context and the way in which help is provided which is important. 'Dependent people' (as much of the research and policy debates refer to disabled people) are socially constructed as such by the circumstances in which help is, or is not, available.

- The quality of someone's life is not determined by the presence or absence of physical impairment but by the nature and quality of the assistance provided to enable someone to go about their daily lives.

A further point has started to emerge from the research material, namely the importance to some disabled women of looking after others – whether it is children or other adults. This part of disabled women's experience has remained unrecognized by most of the feminist research on caring and is more fully examined in the next section of this article.

Disabled women as care-givers

Among those people interviewed who were living outside residential care, a quarter (all women) could be described as care-givers themselves. Some looked after young children, some provided assistance to a disabled partner, while others provided support to a parent. These were all women who needed help with daily living tasks themselves and the only reason that they were able to provide help to others was that they lived in a physical environment which suited their needs, they had access to transport and they received appropriate help themselves, over which they had control.

When people have control over the way that personal assistance is given they are able to become care-givers themselves if they so choose. As being a

FEMINIST REVIEW NO 51, AUTUMN 1995

woman in our society is so tied up with care-giving, the ability to use personal assistance in this way is obviously very important to many disabled women. For example, the availability of personal assistance made it possible for Rachel to look after her mother when she had a stroke.

My mother died two and a half years ago and if it hadn't been for volunteers [from whom Rachel receives personal assistance] I wouldn't have been able to enable her to live at home for as long as she did. Due to her stroke she became disabled herself and I had to keep a continual eye on her, make sure her bills were paid, her washing was done. Occasionally if the home help didn't turn up, or Meals on Wheels didn't turn up I had to prepare her meals for her and so on. She needed a lot of prompting and reminding that certain things had to be done and some days she would be more confused than others and then when the help she needed became more physical there is no way I could have carried on helping her without the volunteers. She would have had to stay in hospital if I hadn't had the volunteers whereas after her last stroke she was able to come out and she lived for another four months at home.

If a disabled mother is physically to look after her small child and not have to hand over this responsibility to someone else, it is necessary for her to be able to direct the personal assistance she requires. Moira employs personal assistants (using a cash grant made by her social services authority) and emphasizes the importance of being able to direct her personal assistance in a way which enabled her to be her daughter's primary care-giver.

I first got PAs when Molly was very small . . . I didn't want my mother doing the things that I would have done . . . I didn't want Molly running to her instead of to me and it would have been difficult for her to stop that happening if at the same time she was going to have a normal relationship as a grandmother to Molly. So that's when I got the money off the Council to employ people and I could tell them exactly what to do . . . you know, like if she fell over and hurt herself then they were to pick her up and put her on my lap so it was me that did the kissing better. And of course Molly was fond of my PAs, but it was always clear that I was her mother.

Jackie is parenting within a lesbian relationship and has not been able to get adequate practical assistance to enable her to establish and maintain her own relationship with two-year-old Dan. She talked about how

the thing I was upset about is just the fact that we're [Jackie and Ros] so glued together. Like my relationship with Dan is practically totally dependent on Ros so my ability to have separate time, a separate relationship with Dan is not there, and Ros's ability to have her own life is pretty non-existent as well.

Having been refused help from her local social services department – who will only provide assistance with personal care tasks – Jackie has enlisted the help of friends but with varying degrees of success. She described how one friend was willing to help but acted in such a way that her own relationship with Dan got in the way of Jackie's relationship with him.

> There was one time when I got so fed up with her that I stormed out of the room and then stormed back in and said if you're looking after Dan I'm going out. So I went off out and when I came back Dan was in bed and we actually talked about it. I realised that part of the problem was that I didn't trust her on the issue of supporting me as a disabled mother and not being a stupid, taking-over, able-bodied, not-a-brain-cell-in-the-head person.

Their talk helped, as Jackie went on to describe – 'because she understands more she's worked out her own way of doing it which is more supportive of me'.

Sometimes, the physical environment in which a woman lives can be a barrier to looking after others. Maeve lives in a three-bedroom house but cannot manage the stairs so her 9-year-old daughter sleeps downstairs with her. Maeve's husband has left and her sons (aged 21 and 17) do not provide her with much help at all, although the younger one receives the Invalid Care Allowance for supposedly providing assistance to his mother (an equivalent amount of money is deducted from Maeve's own benefits). She gets no help from health or social services. 'I don't get a home help at all now. The home help I had she went into hospital herself so I haven't had one since then. My ironing in there is just up to here.'

Maeve has been trying to get an electric wheelchair so that she could take her daughter out and also take her to school, but has had no success so far.

> An electric chair now that would make a difference, obviously you would have so much more independence. But nothing's happened about that . . . I was at the MS Society only last week, they have offered me a grant but it's not enough to pay for one. It'd be great, it would be such a sense of independence.

While many disabled women choose to be care-givers, the experience – particularly if other sources of help are not available – can inhibit their own attempts to assert independence in their lives. Bina's experience, for example, is of a lack of outside help significantly inhibiting her independence. Bina's personal assistance needs are met by her mother who herself increasingly needs help. 'She has diabetes and she has heart problems. She needs some care, some help with getting into and out of the bath. She is looking after me and I am looking after her.' Bina, who is 47 years old, is torn between, on the one hand, wanting to live independently in housing which is properly adapted to her needs, away from her mother, and on the other hand, the knowledge that her mother needs her. 'I'm very touchy with my mum. It's not that I don't want to be independent, it's that if I leave her, what would happen to her? I get depressed about the difficult situation. I want to leave but on the other hand my mum needs me.' Bina's experience reflects that of many women who are in a reciprocal caring relationship, where each person's autonomy is restricted by the lack of alternative help. Such situations reflect the complexity of many caring relationships and the difficulty of separating out the 'carer' from the 'cared for'.

What all of these interviews illustrate, however, is that caring for others, in the sense of giving emotional and physical support, is part of human relationships. Disabled women are often prevented from participating in such relationships because they do not receive appropriate help and/or live in an inappropriate physical environment. In contrast, the provision of accessible housing and equipment, and of personal assistance over which they have control, enables disabled women to participate in the kind of relationships – with all their dilemmas, joys and sorrows – that nondisabled people take for granted.

Disabled women and community care policies

Qualitative research – and associated policy analysis – can have an important impact on those who are, or who will be in the future, health and social services professionals, politicians and policy-makers. If such research merely confirms the assumption that disabled people are in the category of 'them' rather than 'us' by refusing to incorporate our subjective reality and colluding with the belief that our lives are not worth living, then this research will do nothing to further our human and civil rights and much to promote prejudice against us.

The subjective reality of disabled people needs, therefore, to be fully represented within sociological research. Feminist researchers – with their particular aim of 'creating a space for an absent subject' – have a clear responsibility for ensuring that disabled women's voices are heard. The research on which this article is based aimed to express the experiences of women (and men) whose physical impairments mean that they need help with going about their daily life and, in so doing, illustrated that community care policy and practice often fails to promote or protect disabled women's human and civil rights.

Feminist research on 'informal carers' has colluded with the assumption that there is a neat division within households between those who need help with daily living tasks, and are 'dependent', and those who give help and are 'carers'. Yet none of those people whom I interviewed referred to family members who helped them as 'carers'. Instead, they talked about 'my mother', 'my husband', 'my partner'. They talked about their relationships not about their 'carers'. Moreover, it is clear many disabled people – but particularly disabled women – experience relationships with partners, children, parents where they give physical and/or emotional support.

The social construction of 'informal carers', and in particular the assumption that caring is about taking charge of someone, diminishes relationships. Rather than assuming that the presence of a disabled family member creates a relationship of carer and cared-for, it is the relationship between partners, parent and child, siblings, etc., which should be recognized. Some relationships can sustain the giving of personal assistance, some cannot. Some people can facilitate independence for their partner, parent or child, some cannot. Some relationships are abusive and exploitative, some are liberating. To categorize people as carers and dependants is to gloss over all of this. It is also to obscure the way in which gender inequalities may be a key determinant of disabled women's access to control over the help that they need.

Independent living for many disabled women means the right to the help and housing they require in order to play a full role within their household and within personal relationships, as well as the opportunity to work outside the home and engage in social, leisure and political activities.

When feminists challenge the sexual division of labour in the context of childcare, the intention is not that women should cease loving and looking after their children but rather that men should do more of the loving and looking after. Disabled women, particularly those who have personal assistance requirements, are in the position of having to argue for their right to participate in childcare – and indeed in all the other tasks which go to make up running a home. Such a human right cannot be achieved while statutory services fail to recognize the roles that disabled women play within their household, instead treating them as passive recipients of 'informal care'.

State funding of personal assistance is particularly important for disabled women as they are less likely to be able to rely on their own earning power to enable them to purchase the help they need. This is partly because of women's general economic disadvantages but also because impairment for women is less likely to be a result of either industrial injury or traumatic accidents (which causes may result in compensatory benefits or cash payments) than it is for men. In contrast women's experience of impairment is more likely to be associated with chronic conditions or illness (such as arthritis) or with old age, both of which situations are themselves associated with poverty.

FEMINIST REVIEW NO 51, AUTUMN 1995

The most common form of collective provision of personal assistance – statutory services determined by professional perceptions and priorities – is often part of women's experience of oppression in that services are delivered in ways which do not recognize the role which women play within their households, nor their wish to participate fully in personal relationships and in society. On the other hand, having the money to purchase assistance clearly promotes women's ability to participate in personal relationships and in the wider society. Moreover, while the experience of statutory services often means that the needs of Black women and lesbians are not met, having control over how assistance is given means that women can ensure that such assistance meets their particular needs.

Conclusion

Nasa Begum, in her research on women's experience of receiving personal assistance, concluded:

> The issues that nondisabled women have to confront in relation to power, sexuality, body image and so on become particularly ferocious when confronted in the private domain of the personal care situation. A lack of power, control and choice over how one's basic needs are met leaves [disabled women] at the mercy of others, compromising and negotiating for the things other people take for granted every day. The costs of receiving personal care can be astronomical both in emotional and practical terms.

(Begum, 1990: 79)

There is much work yet to do before disabled women have the opportunity of exercising their human and civil rights. Feminist research can help to create the space for their absent voice, joining with the disabled people's movement to bring about changes in the way that resources are used, ensuring that personal assistance needs are met in a way which promotes disabled people's full participation in society.

Notes

Jenny Morris is a freelance researcher and author of *Pride Against Prejudice: Transforming Attitudes to Disability* and *Independent Lives: Community Care and Disabled People*. She also edited *Able Lives?: Women's Experience of Paralysis* and *Alone Together: Voices of Single Mothers*. She has compiled a collection of writings by disabled feminists entitled *Feminism and Disability*, published by The Women's Press.

With thanks to Nasa Begum and Lois Keith for their comments on this article.

References

BALWIN, S. and TWIGG, J. (1991) 'Women and community care: reflections on a debate', in McClean, M. and Groves, D. (1991) editors, *Women's Issues in Social Policy* London: Routledge.

BEGUM, Nasa (1990) *The Burden of Gratitude: Women with Disabilities Receiving Personal Care* Warwick: University of Warwick and SCA.

BRISENDEN, Simon (1989) 'A charter for personal care', in *Progress*, 16, Disablement Income Group.

DALLEY, Gillian (1988) *Ideologies of Caring: Rethinking Community and Collectivism* Basingstoke: Macmillan.

FINCH, Janet (1990) 'The Politics of Community Care in Britain' in Ungerson, C. (1990) editor, *Gender and Caring: Work and Welfare in Britain and Scandinavia* Hemel Hempstead: Harvester Wheatsheaf.

FINCH, Janet and GROVES, Dulcie (1983) *A Labour of Love: Women, Work and Caring* London: Routledge & Kegan Paul.

GRAHAM, Hilary (1983) 'Caring: a labour of love', in **Finch** and **Groves** (1983).

—— (1991) 'The concept of caring in feminist research: the case of domestic service' *Sociology* Vol. 25, No. 1: 61–78.

KEITH, Lois (1992) 'Who cares wins? Women, caring and disability' *Disability, Handicap and Society* Vol. 7, No. 2: 167–75.

MASON, Philip (1992) 'The representation of disabled people: a Hampshire Centre for Independent Living Discussion Paper' *Disability, Handicap and Society* Vol. 7, No. 1: 79–84.

MORRIS, Jenny (1989) editor, *Able Lives: Women's Experience of Paralysis* London: The Women's Press.

—— (1991) *Pride Against Prejudice: Transforming Attitudes to Disability* London: The Women's Press.

—— (1993a) *Community Care or Independent Living?* York: Joseph Rowntree Foundation.

—— (1993b) *Independent Lives? Community Care and Disabled People* Basingstoke: Macmillan.

OLIVER, Michael (1991) *The Politics of Disablement* Basingstoke: Macmillan.

OPCS (1988) *OPCS Surveys of Disability in Great Britain: Report 2, The Financial Circumstances of Disabled Adults Living in Private Households* London: HMSO.

RADAR and ARTHRITIS CARE (1991) *The Right to a Clean Home* London: RADAR and Arthritis Care.

SMITH, Dorothy (1988) *The Everyday World as Problematic: A Feminist Sociology* Milton Keynes: Open University Press.

WALMSLEY, Jan (1993) 'Contradictions in caring: reciprocity and interdependence' *Disability, Handicap and Society* Vol. 8, No. 2: 129–42.

Imagining (the) Difference:

Gender, Ethnicity and Metaphors of Nation

Maureen Molloy

FEMINIST REVIEW NO 51, AUTUMN 1995, pp. 94–112

Abstract

This article critiques the way in which three feminist authors reinscribe traditional liberal values when seeking new ways of thinking about the nation. It suggests that in rejecting affective or embodied metaphors, such as community or kinship, the authors fall into the trap of reinscribing values which have historically excluded women and ethnic or racial minorities from full participation in the polity. The article argues for a rejection of the affect/rationality model which underpins these arguments and suggests that new metaphors for the nation will emerge as those who have been excluded claim a place in the polity.

Keywords

difference; gender; ethnicity; politics; nation; body

Communities are to be distinguished, not by their falsity/genuineness, but by the style in which they are imagined.

(Anderson, 1991: 6)

If we are to take Benedict Anderson at his word we can argue that contemporary New Zealand is currently undergoing a process of re-imagining. There are at least two alternative visions being proposed and contested. One powerful re-imagining has wrenched the country from its social democratic heritage and envisions it as an agglomeration of competitive, profit-making individuals and corporate groups surviving or perishing by virtue of their efficiencies, daring and ability to generate market niches (Crocombe *et al.*, 1991; James, 1992). Another re-imagining draws on a different history. It is anchored in the Treaty of Waitangi, a treaty between the British Crown and Maori peoples, signed first in the Bay of Islands in February 1840 (Orange, 1987) and reiterated in the creation of four Maori seats in Parliament in 1867. In contemporary terms it is an imagining of a polity based primarily on two cultures, recognized within a single state in the context of an increasingly culturally diverse national population. The first imagining reduces us all to the same kind of being –

enterprising, individualistic, competitive, profit-hunting. The second argues definitively for the recognition and institutionalization of difference.

Although New Zealand seems now to find itself most commonly noted in the international literature for its rightist economic programme, it has, perhaps paradoxically, also undergone a radical change in terms of its recognition of the claims for social justice over the past ten years. Arguably, the most significant of these changes is the 1985 amendment to the Treaty of Waitangi Act which allowed grievances and claims dating back to 1840 to be considered and rectified.[1] In 1987 a High Court decision on a case brought by the New Zealand Maori Council against the Crown gave quasi-constitutional status to the Treaty and legal weight to the concept of a partnership between Maori and the Crown (Kawharu, 1989: xii). Since 1985 there have been several hundred claims filed with the Treaty of Waitangi Tribunal and a number of momentous settlements have been reached, including a settlement of all fisheries claims. Beyond its implications as a basis for re-claiming land and resources, the Treaty has become a 'foundation document' and commitment to recognizing its principles is now written into the charters of universities, schools and other social institutions. Legislation is now subject to consideration as to how it fulfils or fails to fulfil Treaty principles.[2]

Other significant events have followed. Homosexuality was decriminalized in a storm of controversy in 1985. In 1990 the New Zealand Parliament adopted a Bill of Rights which prohibited discrimination on the basis of sex, race, ethnicity, age, religion, disability or marital status and in 1993 the Bill was amended to include sexual orientation. Among the shortest-lived legislation was the Pay Equity Act (1990), the Labour government's attempt to adjust historical differences between men's and women's wages, repealed by the newly elected National Government at the end of the same year. In November 1993 the nation voted to change its electoral system from a 'first past the post' system, in which the party with the most members elected forms the government, to Mixed Member Proportional Representation, based on the West German model. Under this system coalition governments are virtually inevitable and the number of Maori seats in Parliament will depend on the numbers of voters registered on the Maori electoral roll. During that election the first Pacific Island Member of Parliament was elected and Sandra Lee became the first Maori woman elected to a general (as opposed to Maori) seat. Shortly after the election Helen Clark became the first female leader of a major political party and the first female Leader of the Opposition.

These changes have taken place within the context of an increasingly culturally diverse national population. At the end of the Second World War

FEMINIST REVIEW NO 51, AUTUMN 1995

Maori accounted for 5.8 per cent of the population, while those of European extraction (commonly referred to as pakeha) accounted for 93.6 per cent. Since the 1960s, immigration to New Zealand from the Pacific nations of Samoa, Tonga, Niue, Tokelau and Fiji has led to the establishment of Pacific Island communities which now include a significant proportion of New Zealand-born adults and children. As of the 1991 census, Pacific Islanders comprised 3.7 per cent of the population and Auckland is now the largest Polynesian city in the world. Between the 1986 and 1991 censi the number of New Zealanders of Chinese or Indian ethnicity doubled. These two groups now account for about 2 per cent of New Zealand's population. Depending on the criteria used, the Maori population of New Zealand now forms 10 to 14 per cent of the total while those of European extraction account for about 80 to 84 per cent (*New Zealand Official Yearbook 1993*: 79, Table 4.15).[3] The demographic, legislative and economic changes of the past ten years have been both paradoxical and controversial. The impact and advisability of immigration, questions about whether New Zealand can or must be bicultural, or multicultural, and the extent to which Maori claims should be settled before issues of multiculturalism are addressed are the subject of private and public debate (Awatere, 1984; Spoonley, 1993; Spoonley and Hirsh, 1990; Walker, 1990).

New Zealand is not, of course, unique in its political struggles over to what extent difference or group rights can or should be institutionalized within structures of governance. Rearticulating democratic theory is an urgent concern in the light of 'ethnic' balkanization going on all over the world. Bloody conflicts in Eastern Europe and Africa and ongoing constitutional crises in Canada testify to the need of contemporary democratic states to incorporate the majority of their national populations who have to date been excluded from full citizenship. In Australia the landmark Mabo decision recognized Aboriginal Australian customary claims to land and is forcing a nation which has only recently begun to see itself as multi-cultural to come to terms with centuries of injustice to Aboriginal peoples (Butt, 1993).[4] Worldwide these political struggles have generated a fluorescence of scholarly theorizing. Political theorists faced with the convincing documentation of the racist and sexist genesis of liberal democracies are trying now to theorize or imagine new forms of political participation and identify the values and processes on which they might be based, values such as difference, diversity and multiplicity (Benhabib and Cornell, 1987; LaClau and Mouffe, 1985; Minow, 1990). Prominent among these scholars have been a number of feminists who have argued that the individual upon whom liberal democratic theory is based is in fact a male individual with a male body (Benhabib, 1987; Pateman, 1988). They have argued for the necessity of a new imagining which recognizes differences between male and female and does not take male experience as normative or neutral.

Anne Phillips has argued that much feminist political theory 'identified false oppositions, dualisms or dichotomies as the characteristics of orthodox, masculine thought, and yet so much of it reads like straightforward reversals of what previous writers have said' (Phillips, 1993: 52). In this article I examine aspects of work by three feminist writers, Iris Marion Young, Anna Yeatman and Sneja Gunew, which do not fall into the pattern of reversal but which, instead, seem to be reinscribing traditional liberal hierarchies. Yeatman, Young and Gunew are not, in the work considered in this article, concerned so much with structures and institutions of the state, as they are with the imaginings which inform those institutions. Each proposes alternative models or imaginings which, she argues, will enhance the ability of contemporary nation-states and those groups within them making claims for social justice to accommodate, and indeed support, difference. However, the models they propose seem to me to be highly problematic as models which affirm difference. There is, I think, a contradiction between the way in which 'difference' is theorized in these works and the life-ways and values of people whose interests a politics of difference is presumed to advance. In the current political context in New Zealand these writers offer a chance to reflect on the implications of particular theoretical models for how the imagining of the polity can be effected in practice.

Iris Marion Young has been one of the most influential theorists of difference as diversity. In articles (Young, 1989; 1990a) and in her book *Justice and the Politics of Difference* (1990) Young attempts to articulate both the philosophical foundations and pragmatic schema for a politics of diversity. For Young justice must involve both the public affirmation of group difference and institutional structures for group representation in public decision-making. Young builds her theory of difference around the notion of a 'social group' which she defines as 'a collective of persons differentiated from at least one other group by cultural forms, practices or way of life' (Young, 1990: 43). She distinguishes social groups from other kinds of human collectivities using Heidegger's concept of throwness: 'one *finds oneself* as a member of a group, which one experiences as always already having been' (Young, 1990: 46 [emphasis in original]). One does not choose, then, to be a member of a group but must, presumably, be born into it: '[g]roups . . . constitute individuals. A person's particular sense of history, affinity, and separateness, even the person's mode of reasoning, evaluating, and expressing feeling, are constituted partly by her or his group affinities' (Young, 1990: 45).

FEMINIST REVIEW NO 51, AUTUMN 1995

Young's examples of social groups include 'women and men, age groups, racial and ethnic groups, [and] religious groups' (1990: 43). She argues that common practices and ways of life give members of a social group 'a specific affinity with one another because of their similar experience' (Young, 1990: 43). She sees this affinity as manifested as common identity and it is common identity which, for Young, is the primary defining attribute of a social group (Young, 1990: 44). Identity is not, however, unitary. She argues for complex, contextualized, linguistically achieved, heterogenous identities which are 'multiple, cross-cutting, fluid, and shifting' (Young, 1990: 48). There is an implicit vector in Young's theory of social groups which proceeds from common experience to affinity to identity. She argues, for example, that '[m]embers of each gender have a certain affinity with others in their group because of what they do or experience, and differentiate themselves from the other gender' (Young, 1990: 43). However, being born into or finding oneself a member of a social group and the common experiences which are generated are not sufficient conditions for group identity. Young argues that social groups exist only in relation to other social groups: 'group identification arises . . . in the encounter and interaction between social collectivities that experience some differences in their way of life and forms of association' (Young, 1990: 43).

Young does privilege ethnicity or 'cultural' difference over other kinds of difference. She argues, for example, that '[g]roup differences of gender, age, and sexuality should not be ignored, but publicly acknowledged and accepted. *Even more so* should group differences of nation or ethnicity be accepted' (Young, 1990: 179 [emphasis mine]). However, in positing a model or metaphor for political groupings Young rejects one of the key concepts usually associated with ethnic or national groups. Specifically, she rejects the notion of 'community' as a useful counter to the atomistic individual which liberal theory privileges. She argues that community, whatever its positive characteristics, functions to suppress and sometimes to repress difference.

> [The ideal of community] expresses a desire for the fusion of subjects with one another which in practice operates to exclude those with whom the group does not identify. The ideal of community denies and represses social difference, the fact that the polity cannot be thought of as a unity in which all participants share a common experience and common values. In its privileging of face-to-face relations, moreover, the ideal of community denies difference in the form of the temporal and spatial distancing that characterizes social process.
>
> (Young, 1990: 227)

While much of Young's critique of 'community' is persuasive, she over-emphasizes the distinction between 'community' and her concept of the 'social group'. By substituting a 'pre-given group', which one experiences as having always already been, Young interposes a requirement for authenticity into the political process. Ideas of the 'naturalness' or 'pre-givenness' of community deflect away from viewing community 'as an ideological and material construction, whose boundaries, structures and norms are a result of constant processes of struggles and negotiations' (Yuval-Davis, 1991: 59). That is, the pre-givenness of the group precludes the kinds of fluxes in identity which Young argues for. Furthermore, the necessity of a group being 'pre-given' reiterates or reinserts many of those implications of 'natural community'. Who gets to decide whether a group is pre-given or not? And what kinds of counter-claims does the necessity for pre-givenness generate within the political process? Finally, there is a whiff, in Young's identification of pre-given social groups, of the anchoring of a politics of identity in an essentialized notion of the body. The groups which Young persistently uses as examples – women, Blacks, the disabled, homosexuals, the aged – are the quintessential 'equity' categories. 'Class', or even 'the poor', is conspicuously absent from her list of social groups, except inasmuch as the above mentioned groups are more likely to be 'the poor'.

As an alternative to 'community' as a model for the polity Young proposes the model of 'the city'. This contrast between 'community' (simple, rural, face to face) and 'city' (complex, urban, anonymous) is one which is well embedded in the modern history of Western social thought (Williams, 1973). Young argues that, in distinction to the suppression of difference associated with notions of community, cities are characterized by variety, unplannedness, contiguity and interaction of strangers and possibilities for new social groupings. The city thus offers a model of social interaction and organization which does not depend on notions of organic wholeness or face-to-face interaction. A normative ideal of city life, she argues, suggests social differentiation without exclusion, variety, eroticism and public arenas for 'unassimilated otherness'.

In marked contradistinction to Young's experientially 'pre-given' groups, Anna Yeatman theorizes identity as arising out of a contestation between the 'guardians' of policy and those who are excluded (Yeatman, 1993). The question of who or what defines politically salient difference is thus, for Yeatman, a matter of history and negotiation. She doesn't, therefore, privilege one kind of 'difference' over another. Furthermore, she argues that seeing identity as 'pre-given' closes down emancipatory politics. She argues instead for the analysis of speaking positions which are grounded, not in the individual's identity, but in her relation (as privileged guardian, as excluded, as representative) to the policies being contested.

FEMINIST REVIEW NO 51, AUTUMN 1995

Unlike Young, Yeatman retains the notion of a national community which the 'state is designed to protect, regulate, and advance' (Yeatman, 1994: 92). The problem for Yeatman is the contestation between different and competing notions of how this 'national community' is constituted. Like Young she draws on a traditional distinction in Western thought to characterize two models of the national community, in this case Henry Maine's (1867) distinction between societies in which social interaction is based on status, that is fixed positions within a social system, and those societies in which interaction is based on contract between two equal parties. Yeatman identifies the two predominant models of the national community in Western democracies as the customary model and the conventional model. The customary model 'is structured in terms of the logic of kinship . . . [a]ll those who come under the nation are understood to be its children because they share in a community of descent' (Yeatman, 1994: 94). In line with this metaphor of kinship the state based on this customary model is gendered in terms of its welfare, work and war policies. She argues that customary models of the state are based on 'culturally exclusive accounts of community and the kinds of undemocratic practice such exclusion justifies' (Yeatman, 1994: 17).

Yeatman's alternative to kinship as the metaphor of the national community is a conventionalist model. Under this model the nation has a 'legal-conventionalist view of how its members came together and what legally-sanctioned values they must have in common . . . [These include] values like equal opportunity, anti-discrimination, equity, equality, due process, natural justice, individual right to participation, and the like' (Yeatman, 1994: 95). She argues '[t]his community is one which has to have clear legal-juridical boundaries which determine who belongs and who does not, but it does not depend on the idea of being based in a mutually exclusive kinship community' (Yeatman, 1994: 95). For Yeatman this is the self-made national community which sees itself as 'independent', 'self-determining', and its orientation to action is 'rational', 'empirical', 'pragmatic' and 'unheroic' (Yeatman, 1994: 100-01).

Yeatman and Young end up in different, but, I would argue, differently contradictory, places in their respective rejections of metaphors of kinship and community for the polity. Both in some sense recognize 'culture' and 'culturally distinctive groups' as units around which a politics of difference must be built, although Yeatman does not privilege ethnicity as Young does. Their concern is how groups can articulate to processes of governing to achieve a form of democratic pluralism. However, the implications of the 'internal' constitution of social groups for the constitution of the national polity is not adequately considered. Both see 'identity', however complex, as somehow key to the constitution of social groups. Yet, both argue that the nation-state as a whole must identify itself in terms which exclude apparently affective notions, such as kinship and community. Affinity and identity constitute subnational groups, but these notions cannot spill over into the national or formal governmental level.

These disavowals of affect seem to me to be very problematic in formulating new models or metaphors for the polis, especially when claims are being made by groups in which ethnicity and polity are articulated through kinship, when the public and the private, the polity and the family and even the community, are not separate, but are, at times at least, one and the same. The models of kinship being rejected here are models which see the family as an exclusive and bounded group – a little commonwealth in which those who belong are kin and those who do not are enemies (a version of kinship it must be said which owes much more to Locke and Rousseau than, for example, to Levi-Strauss). For groups in which the polity and the kin-group are substantially the same entity this opposing of metaphors of kinship and metaphors of rational action is highly problematic, seemingly reiterating the old oppositions between 'primitive' and 'civilized' societies.

In New Zealand, Maori claims for justice are anchored in the recognition of kin-based claims to land, fisheries and other *taonga* (treasures). One must ask what meaning models of the state which disavow these affective values can have for those whom the traditional liberal models of individual rights have excluded. For those making claims, kinship and community are not just metaphors of exclusion, nor are they experienced only as oppressive. The commitments to kin and community are in some sense held to be the central values of *Maoritanga*[5] or, equally, of *fa'a Samoa*.[6] In New Zealand arguments against kinship and community as central values in political process may act to delegitimize indigenous and minority political structures and claims. At best, the models posed by Yeatman and Young confine indigenous values to the subnational level, but preclude them from defining the polity.

A related problem occurs in Sneja Gunew's consideration of the positive revaluing of 'race' by groups making claims for political and cultural autonomy. While Young and Yeatman are concerned with how the polis or the nation is to be imagined, Gunew looks critically at how claims are made by those marginalized by the dominant culture. Gunew's problem is a serious one – why race and ethnicity are constantly conflated in political debate and what pitfalls are inherent in the positive use of 'race' by subordinated peoples making claims for justice (Gunew, 1993: 2, 10). She traces the shifting ontologies of 'race' and 'ethnicity': the association of race with the biological and its falling from favour in terms of the more self-identified 'ethnicity'. However, she notes and problematizes the recent reclamation of 'race' as an identity marker for groups wishing 'to resist assimilation and pursue cultural difference and autonomy' (Gunew, 1993: 10). She argues that for these groups 'race' 'holds the magic of irreducible difference, a non-negotiable space which heralds a separate history'. However she argues that this history is 'no less phantasmatic at its edges . . . than all histories' (Gunew, 1993: 10). Gunew is concerned about the way in which this reclaiming of race is 'tied in disturbing ways to the notion of primordial rights to land', disturbing because of the historical and contemporary coincidence of the blood-land link and fascism. For Gunew the emphasis must shift away from 'race' with its implications of biological fixity towards an understanding of distinctive cultures and lifeways. 'It[7] is not', she states 'a matter of *Blut und Boden*, blood and territory, but of ethos, that is, the characteristic spirit . . . of a people or community' (Gunew, 1993: 17).

There is much in this analysis which strikes a chord and much, also, which disturbs. We have an obligation to oppose fascism and to be relentlessly critical of the ideologies which contribute to its rise. It is important, however, not to overstate the importance of primordialism or to be confused about the ontologies of fascism. Historically at least as many atrocities have been committed and justified by a theory of superior use and therefore use-rights, as by primordial links. Claims to land tend to swing back and forth between claims of prime or prior occupation, spiritual connexion and superior usage. The terminological shift from 'native' or 'indigenous' to 'First Peoples' reflects the emphasis on primacy, as did European settler claims that Australia and British Columbia were *terrae nullii* – empty lands with no (legitimate) owners (Cail, 1974; Gelder and Jacobs, 1995; Richardson, 1994). Colonizers' claims were also commonly based on superior use – that is that the indigenous occupiers did not use the land effectively or use it at all. This argument was not, of course, invented in the colonies but was well developed during the enclosures in England and the Highland clearances (Richards, 1982). Coalitions between contemporary ecology and indigenous movements often mobilize all three claims – prior or first occupancy, spiritual connexion and superior (i.e., sustainable) usage (see, for example, Jacobs, 1994, for an account of the interaction between the feminist, ecology and aboriginal rights movements in Australia).

While one might be sceptical of the romanticization which sometimes underpins these contemporary coalitions, Gunew's counterposing of blood and territory on the one hand and the spirit of the people on the other, seems to me to be highly problematic and contradictory to the general theoretical position she is taking. In the first place, she reinscribes the old body/mind, material/spiritual dichotomy which has been the target of post-colonial and feminist theory. Furthermore, the separation of spirit from land derives from an attitude to land which sees it as a thing, a material resource to be used. Maori claims to land invoke a different set of relations between bodies, land and spirits. The word for 'land' and 'placenta' is the same – *'whenua'*. *'Hapu'* means both 'pregnant' and a localized subtribal group. In a history of Maori–pakeha relations in New Zealand after the land wars of the 1860s Keith Sinclair documents the persistent refusal of Tawhiao, a chief of the Waikato, to settle with the British government which wished to substitute other land for that which had been confiscated from his people. In addition to the new territory Tawhiao was offered substantial sums of money and limited governmental autonomy. He refused the offer: the land offered was not substitutable for the land of his people and, as Sinclair comments, he 'lost his land, but kept his mana'[8] (Sinclair, 1991). Tawhiao's ties to his specific land could not be reduced to simple economic interest, commodification or imperialistic intent.

This mental/material divide underpins Gunew's analysis. She begins her argument about race and ethnicity by comparing the evolution of the terms to the sex/gender distinction. Like sex, race has been seen as 'biology' in contrast to ethnicity (and gender) which is seen as socio-cultural. She cites the work of Gatens (1989) and Grosz (1994) to argue that 'the body is as much an inscribed terrain as any other signifying system. The old body and spirit distinction no longer holds' (Gunew, 1993: 8). However, if bodies are discursively constituted, it follows that they are experienced and enacted in very different ways depending on the cultural and historical position of different subjects (Kirby, 1994). Histories of colonization, for example, are rife with accounts of people who simply declined and died when separated from land and/or kin (see Richards, 1985; Sutton, 1985). Embodied experiences of culturally different subjects must involve different systems of boundaries and differentiations. Furthermore, the imbrication of place, ancestors, spirits and bodies, although discursively constructed (if you like) is also real.

If there is irreducible difference, perhaps it is found here, in this particular cathexis. The phantasm of the ancestor or spirit in the land is not illusion but lived reality. Historian Judith Binney describes such as occasion:

> The dead and the living share this world in Maori thought, and that link remains unbroken. When we first brought a photograph of Pinepine Te Rika [prophet Rua Kenana's] wife, to Materoa Roberts, whom Pinepine had mothered, Materoa lamented and sang directly to the photograph. She talked to Pinepine as though she was with us in the room. We were all momentarily in the presence of her tipuna [ancestor].

(Binney, 1989: 23)

FEMINIST REVIEW NO 51, AUTUMN 1995

In 1980 Materoa Roberts described her relation to Maungapohatu, the sacred mountain of the Tuhoe people to which Pinepine and Rua had been summoned by Archangel Gabriel in 1905.

> I've never been there but my dream has been up there. I saw the place where it is and the way to go. I know the way to go and I know that that mountain is a woman . . . Nobody has told me what I saw. I know what I saw. I suppose that's why I've got a sore back, so I won't go up there. You know, I really want to go up but I'm frightened to go . . . it's not for me to go up that mountain, it's not for me. . . . I talked with [Pinepine] and I told that old lady 'So and so's going to happen, and you're going to be so and so', and it's all come true. That's why Rua told the people, 'If anyone "talks" [foretells], it doesn't matter if it's a kid, listen'.
>
> (Quoted in Binney, 1989: 27)

In this passage Materoa's body (a sore back that prevents her from going where she is not supposed to go), the spirit of God and the ancestors, foretelling, dreaming, and 'second sight', and the mountain are all part of a complex which set her and her people in a determinate relation to each other, to the past and the future. It is arguably not a relation in which land and blood can be set in opposition to 'the spirit of the people'. The spirit of the people is indissoluble from the place and the body, as well as in the dreams and visions.

Gunew is ambivalent about the relations of dreams, visions and phantasms to histories. While seeing separate histories as 'phantasmatic at the edges' she more positively values 'phantasmagoric' myths of origin that locate identity in language or 'the mother tongue' (Gunew, 1993: 10). The OED defines 'phantasm' as 'illusion, phantom, illusive likeness supposed vision of absent (living or dead) person' and 'phantasmagoric' as a 'shifting scene of real or imagined figures.' These definitions are imbued with ambiguities about reality and illusion. If histories are phantasmatic, why only at the edges? Only 'at the edges' leaves open the possibility of a core, 'real', unillusive, unshifting history. The question then is who sees the core and who the phantasm?

If Gunew appears to support cultural difference while denying its 'realities', Young performs a similar operation on sexual difference. 'The social groups, men and women', she boldly iterates, 'are created by the sexual division of labour' (Young, 1990: 43), neatly side-stepping a number of questions about language, the body and subjectivity which have been exercising feminist scholars for years. Instead she reverts to a crude materialism to explain the genesis of gender differentiation; one, it must be said, which sits more comfortably with her emphasis on experience as constitutive of identity than those theorists who emphasize language, the body and the unconscious.

Even more damning, in the light of her own theorizing, is her lack of engagement with how these categories of difference are mutually constituting. Her emphasis is on the similarities in the ways in which 'Others' are constituted within Western epistemologies. Paradoxically, she founds her model of 'difference' on a purposefully neutral, all-encompassing, empty category – the social group. She sets up gender, race/ethnicity/nation, age, religion, and sexual orientation as more or less equivalent categories. She tends to present these as litanies – 'racism, sexism, homophobia, ageism and ableism'; 'women, Blacks, Jews, homosexuals, old people, the mad and feebleminded'; 'race, gender, religion, age, or ethnic identification'. Conceptually the result is a kind of questionnaire approach to difference which fails to take account of how these categories are differently constituted and, particularly, how they mutually constitute or undercut each other.

Theorists as diverse as Foucault (1990), Mosse (1985) and Pateman (1988) have demonstrated how central discourses on sexuality and gender have been to the founding of modern Western societies and nation-states. This is not surprising. Much has been made of Anderson's argument that nations are 'imagined communities' in which ties between members are conceptualized as ties of kinship. Yet gender and kinship are not separate domains of culture but are mutually constituting (Yanigisako and Collier, 1987; Levi-Strauss, 1969; Rubin, 1974). While Young uses Mosse to examine this process in Western societies she does not refer to the literature which examines these issues with reference to non-Western cultures (see, for example, Mohanty, Russo and Torres, 1991; Parker et al., 1992; Sagari and Vaid, 1990).

In privileging national and/or ethnic identity Young imbues it with a kind of ahistorical purity. Yet nationalisms are particular historical formations, deeply gendered from the outset. Chatterjee (1990), for example, argues that nationalisms define 'the political' as such and are premised on an inside/outside dichotomy which metonymically places women/hearth/home inside and at the defining centre of 'the nation':

> by mobilizing the inner/outer distinction against the 'outerness' of the West, nationalist rhetoric makes 'woman' the pure and ahistorical signifier of 'interiority'. In the fight against the enemy from the outside, something within gets even more repressed and 'woman' becomes the mute but necessary allegorical ground for the transactions of nationalist history.
>
> (Radhakrishnan, 1992: 84)

Privileging ethnicity and national identity, without questioning how these identities are often constructed on the basis of repressive gender regimes, leaves women in the trap of betraying their 'community' or 'traditional values' when they assert their need or desire for change (Trinh, 1989). Hierarchy is a central feature of most cultural systems and a general theory of 'difference' which sees different differences as 'equivalent' or additive has the effect of rendering culture as something laudable or at best, neutral. This is a view of culture unlikely to shed much light on the position of women or to aid in their emancipatory projects.

One of the problems with this literature seems to lie with the title of the work which has inspired much rethinking of the polity, Benedict Anderson's *Imagined Communities* (1991). The idea that communities are imagined seems to suggest that things imagined are not real. There is implicit in much of this work a real/representation split which enables Young to repudiate the notion of community while investing the even more nebulous 'social group' with much of its definitional content and Gunew to counterpose land and ethos as if they were a universal opposition and by opposing them the boundary between racist aggression and ethnic self-determination was somehow rendered less problematic. It allows Yeatman to regard notions of kinship as problematic for the national imaginary while seeing rationalism, pragmatism and empiricism as somehow outside that problematic, despite years of feminist critique of the imperialist and masculinist bases of those values. Vicki Kirby (1994) has argued that signifying inevitably requires recourse to a 'real'. Each of these authors in different ways presents one alternative ('community', 'kinship', 'primordial links') as less 'real', more 'ideological', than the one which she proposes as a 'better', more real alternative.

In attempting to imagine a 'politics of difference' Young, Yeatman and Gunew have all, intentionally or not, privileged traditional liberal values associated with Western masculine subjects. This is a movement away from earlier feminist models of the polity which tended to emphasize values associated with femininity – nurturance, caring and sociality. Part of the feminist reaction against affective concepts has been prompted by attempts by the New Right to mobilize them for conservative ends (Else, 1992). The spectacular demise of the recent traditional family values campaign in Britain and the stuttering and unsuccessful attempts in New Zealand to invoke family values in the service of rightist economic policies might signal to us that these two political motifs sit very uneasily with each other. 'Family' and 'community' values do not unproblematically serve the interests of rightist economics. It may be time to reclaim them.

But further than that we need to challenge the way in which this literature swings back and forth between seemingly opposing models: (oppressive) community versus (unoppressive)[9] city; culturally exclusive kinship versus the rational, self-made (inclusive) state; 'the spirit of the people' versus the material of 'blood and land'. Those models based on affect and body are rejected for the impersonal, rational, universal alternatives. The ironies are at least twofold. Firstly, the preferred model of the nation continues to be characterized by traditional Western masculinist values – distance; instrumental engagement; rationality; independence. Secondly, and this is perhaps the more serious irony, this state which is universal, rational and instrumental is made up of units which are constituted by affect – identity and affinity.

It seems to me that it would make more sense to try to undermine the affect/reason duality which underlies these models than to opt, once again, for a traditional model of the nation. As Young points out, although many of us enjoy the privacy, anonymity and diversity of the city, we usually enjoy it in the company of friends, lovers, family and colleagues. There are other models of kinship and community available to us than the oppressive community and the restricted, patriarchal nuclear family. Communities often materialize around people in moments of crisis and celebration. They are as often about defining who has the right to engage in debate as they are about repressing debate altogether. Reconfiguring kin relations has been a major theme of feminism and of most people's daily lives. Single parenting, blended families, gay and lesbian couples, reproductive technologies, *whanau*,[10] fostering – the forms of kinship available to and experienced by a wide variety of people suggest that kinship has immense potential for expressing difference and inclusivity, as well as repression and hierarchy. The point, however, is not that kinship is better than convention or community better than city or that any of these is necessarily better for women. The point is that a good model of a just polity is one which recognizes affect and reason not as separate and separable functions, but as mutually defining aspects of justice.

Perhaps even more important is the fact that the values which propel us to work for a more just form of governance are values which we care for. Although some theorists might argue for more democratic forms of participation or more equitable distribution of resources simply on the grounds of self-interest, a great many people work to change political structures because they care about issues like equity and freedom and they care about the kind of society they inhabit. New Zealand's recent vote to change its Parliamentary system from the traditional British model to Mixed Member Proportional representation (MMP), for example, seems to have been a massive rejection of the undemocratic way in which the country has been governed, particularly in the last ten years of economic 'reform', and a reassertion of the need for politicians to exercise those very qualities that seem often to be forgotten in political theory – co-operation, communication, negotiation. In New Zealand there are calls for a kin-based justice system which would see Maori offenders dealt with within a physical structure and a social framework derived from customary practices (Jackson, 1987–8; 1989). We have seen the creation of a kinship-based youth justice system with the implementation of the Children, Young Persons and their Families Act (1989) in which flexibly defined family groups in consultation with victims develop solutions for dealing with young offenders. These systems call on values which their participants believe in and, when they work, they do so at least in part because of the affective values and ties which are invoked. Movements for political change which base their appeal only on self-interest or rational action are unlikely to engage the hearts and minds of those who have a will to create forms of governance which will support social justice.

We need not remain stuck within traditional Western hierarchies. There are other models or metaphors we can draw on to imagine or theorize the nation. One possibility is that we look to metaphors from the cultures claiming a place in the polity. In New Zealand there is an indigenous model – the *marae*. A *marae* is a structure which is complex and multifunctional. The physical structure consists of an open space for welcoming visitors, a meeting house, an ablutions block and a kitchen/dining hall. *Marae* have rituals for welcoming strangers and incorporating them into the group, and rules of discourse and decision-making (Salmond, 1976; Tauroa and Tauroa, 1986). There are specific roles for both men and women, and, although these have been and continue to be the subject of debate, women do have a legitimate place in the political domain of the *marae* (see Irwin, 1992 for a discussion of women's role on the *marae* and feminist debates about it). Jeff Sissons (1995) has argued that Cook Islands nationalism has been embodied and symbolized in dance. Dances are both structural and processual, involving set moves and individual improvization, group patterns and individual performance, and they usually involve, again, both men and women. As a metaphor for the nation dance is one which might serve to remind us that we are embodied creatures in motion with each other. These are the kind of metaphors which are informing and shifting the imaginaries of south Pacific nations. One would not expect to find them in other regions where different cultures or cultural dynamics are extant.

But finally, perhaps, the point is that as nations work towards the accommodation of difference, the imaginings which inform our visions of the nation, or of the nations which cohabit nation-states, will have to be, like the populations themselves, plural and flexible. Just nations will need to develop flexible imaginaries, plural visions, and multiple metaphors, for that, ultimately is what a politics of difference will demand.

Notes

Maureen Molloy is a senior lecturer in Women's Studies at the University of Auckland, New Zealand. She has published one book, *Those Who Speak to the Heart*, a study of kinship and community change among Highland Scots migrants to New Zealand. She is currently working on a book on popular culture, social policy and professional discourses in New Zealand.

I would like to express my gratitude to the women who over many years have shared their knowledge and friendship with me, in particular the late Millie Witana and Hera Motu, and Anna Baker and Hemo Henare. Nite Fuamatu, Sailau Suaali and Pepe Purcell challenged me to think again about the complex interactions between gender and ethnicity, kinship and community. Meremere Penfold, Judith Binney, Doug Sutton and Heather Worth provided useful commentary on earlier drafts.

1 Under the 1975 Act only grievances dated after the passage of the Act could be considered.

2 Other recent books on the Treaty and its contemporary impacts include Kelsey (1990), McHugh (1991), Sharp (1990), Tauroa (1989).

3 The figures for the Maori population present '[t]hose specifying themselves as half or more New Zealand Maori plus those not specified' (*New Zealand Official Yearbook*, 1993: 79, Table 4.15). Other figures put the Maori population at about 14%.

4 'In 1992 the High Court of Australia found in favour of Eddie Mabo's claim that the 1979 annexation of the Torres Strait was unlawful and in no way extinguished his customary ownership. This decision legitimated Aboriginal prior occupation in Australian Common Law and laid to rest the concept of *terra nullius*, a founding myth of Australian nationhood. Land rights claims, which until this moment had operated within the limits of piecemeal legislation, were now possible across the nation' (Gelder and Jacobs, 1995: 151).

5 Maori culture or the Maori way of life.

6 Samoan culture or 'the Samoan way'.

7 It is not clear what Gunew's 'It' in this sentence refers to.

8 Spiritual power and prestige.

9 In her 1990 paper, 'The ideal of community and the politics of difference', Young contrasted 'community' to the 'unoppressive city', an adjective which she wisely dropped in the chapter of *Justice and the Politics of Difference* (1992) based on this paper.

10 Roughly translated as 'family' or 'extended family', but in practice often including those who might in British kinship terminology be considered friends or colleagues.

References

ANDERSON, B. (1991) *Imagined Communities: Reflections on the Origins and Spread of Nationalisms* London: Verso (revised edition).

ANTHIAS, F. and YUVAL-DAVIS, N. (1989) 'Introduction' in Yuval-Davis, N. and Anthias, F. (1989) editors, *Woman-Nation-State* London: Macmillan.

AWATERE, D. (1984) *Maori Sovereignty* Auckland: Broadsheet.

BENHABIB, S. (1987) 'The generalized and the concrete other: the Kohlberg-Gilligan controversy and feminist theory' in Benhabib and Cornell (1987).

BENHABIB, S. and CORNELL, D. (1987) editors, *Feminism as Critique* Oxford: Basil Blackwell.

BINNEY, J. (1989) 'Some observations on the status of Maori women' *New Zealand Journal of History* Vol. 23.

BUTT, P. and EAGLESON, R. (1993) *Mabo: What the High Court Said* Annandale: Federation Press.

CAIL, R. (1974) *Land, Man and the Law: The Disposal of Crown Lands in British Columbia 1871–1913* Vancouver: University of British Columbia Press.

CHATTERJEE, P. (1990) 'The nationalist resolution of the women's question' in Sagari and Vaid (1990).

CROCOMBE, G., ENRIGHT, M., PORTER, M. with CAUGHEY, T. (1991) *Upgrading New Zealand's Competitive Advantage* Wellington: New Zealand Trade Development Board.

DUPLESSIS, R. *et al.* (1992) editors, *Feminist Voices: Women's Studies Texts for Aotearoa/New Zealand* Auckland and Oxford: Oxford University Press.

ELSE, A. (1992) 'To market and home again: gender and the New Right' in Duplessis *et al.* (1992).

FOUCAULT, M. (1990) *The History of Sexuality* (Vol. 1), Hurley, R., translator, London: Penguin.

GATENS, M. (1989) 'A critique of the sex-gender distinction' in Gunew, S. (1989) editor, *A Reader in Feminist Knowledge* London: Routledge.

GELDER, K. and JACOBS, J. (1995) 'Talking out of place: Authorizing the sacred in postcolonial Australia' *Cultural Studies* Vol. 9, No. 1: 150–60.

GROSZ, E. (1994) *Volatile Bodies: Toward a Corporeal Feminism* Bloomington: Indiana University Press.

GUNEW, S. (1993) 'Feminism and the politics of irreducible differences' in Gunew and Yeatman (1993).

GUNEW, S. and YEATMAN, A. (1993) editors, *Feminism and the Politics of Difference* Sydney: Allen & Unwin.

IRWIN, K. (1992) 'Towards theories of Maori feminism;' in Duplessis *et al.* (1992).

JACKSON, M. (1987–8) *The Maori and the Criminal Justice System: A New Zealand Perspective – He Whaipaanga Hou* Wellington: Policy and Research Division, Department of Justice.

—— (1989) 'A Maori justice system' *Race, Gender, Class* Vol. 9/10.

JACOBS, J. (1994) 'Earth honoring: western desires and indigenous knowledges' in Blunt, A. and Rose, G. (1994) editors, *Writing Women and Space: Colonial and Postcolonial Geographies* New York and London: The Guildford Press.

JAMES, C. (1992) *New Territory: The Transformation of New Zealand, 1984–92* Wellington: Bridget Williams Books.

KAWHARU, H. (1989) editor, *Waitangi: Maori and Pakeha Perspectives of the Treaty of Waitangi* Auckland and Oxford: Oxford University Press.

KELSEY, J. (1990) *A Question of Honour: Labour and the Treaty* Wellington, Boston: Allen & Unwin.

KIRBY, V. (1994) *Corporeographies: the Body at the Scene of Writing* New York: Routledge.

LACLAU, E. and **MOUFFE, C.** (1985) *Hegemony and Socialist Strategy: Towards a Radical Democratic Politics* Moore, W. and Cammack, P., translators, London: Verso.

LEVI-STRAUSS, C. (1969) *The Elementary Structures of Kinship* revised edition, Bell, J. and von Sturnmer, J. translators; Needham, R. editor, London: Eyre & Spottiswoode.

McHUGH, P. (1991) *The Maori Magna Carta* Auckland and Oxford: Oxford University Press.

MAINE, H. (1867) *Ancient Law: Its Connections with the Early History of Society and Its Relation to Modern Ideas* New York: Scribner & Sons.

MINOW, M. (1990) *Making All the Difference* Ithaca: Cornell University Press.

MOHANTY, C., RUSSO, A. and **TORRES, L.** (1991) editors, *Third World Women and the Politics of Feminism* Bloomington: Indiana University Press.

MOSSE, G. (1985) *Nationalism and Sexuality* New York: Howard Fertig.

NEW ZEALAND OFFICIAL YEARBOOK 1993 (96th edition) Wellington: Department of Statistics.

ORANGE, C. (1987) *The Treaty of Waitangi* Wellington: Allen & Unwin, Port Nicholson Press.

PARKER, A., RUSSO, M., SOMMER, D. and **YAEGER, P.** (1992) editors, *Nationalisms and Sexualities* New York and London: Routledge.

PATEMAN, C. (1988) *The Sexual Contract* Stanford: Stanford University Press.

PHILLIPS, A. (1993) *Democracy and Difference* University Park: Pennsylvania State University.

RADHAKRISHNAN, R. (1992) 'Nationalism, gender and the narrative of identity' in **Parker** *et al.* (1992).

RICHARDS, E. (1982) *A History of the Highland Clearances* London: Croom Helm.

—— (1985) 'Highland emigrants to South Australia in the 1850s' Northern Scotland Vol. 5.

RICHARDSON, B. (1994) *People of Terra Nullius: Betrayal and Rebirth in Aboriginal Canada* Vancouver: Douglas McIntyre.

RUBIN, G. (1975) 'The traffic in women: notes on the "political economy" of sex' in Reiter, R. (1975) editor, *Toward an Anthropology of Women* New York and London: Monthly Review Press.

SAGARI, K. and **VAID, S.** (1990) editors, *Recasting Women: Essays in Indian Colonial History* New Brunswick: Rutgers University Press.

SALMOND, A. (1976) *Hui: A Study of Maori Ceremonial Gatherings* Wellington: A. H. & A. W. Reed.

SHARP, A. (1990) *Justice and the Maori: Maori Claims in New Zealand Political Argument in the 1980s* Auckland: Oxford University Press.

SINCLAIR, K. (1991) *Kinds of Peace: Maori People after the Wars, 1870–85* Auckland: Auckland University Press.

SISSONS, J. (1995) 'National movements: Cook Islands dance since self-government' *Sites* Autumn (forthcoming).

SPOONLEY, P. (1993) *Racism and Ethnicity* Auckland and Oxford: Oxford University Press.

SPOONLEY, P. and **HIRSH, W.** (1990) *Between the Lines: Racism and the New Zealand Media* Auckland: Heinemann Reed.

SUTTON, D. (1985) 'The Whence of the Moriori' *New Zealand Journal of History* Vol. 19.

TAUROA, H. (1989) *Healing the Breech: One Maori's Perspective on the Treaty of Waitangi* Auckland: Collins.

TAUROA, H. and **TAUROA, P.** (1986) *Te Marae: a Guide to Customs and Protocol* Auckland: Reed Methuen.

TRINH, M. (1989) *Woman, Native, Other* Bloomington: Indiana University Press.

WALKER, R. (1990) *Ka Whawhai Tonu Matou: Struggle Without End* Auckland and New York: Penguin Books.

WILLIAMS, R. (1973) *The Country and the City* London: Chatto and Windus.

YANIGISAKO, S. and **COLLIER, J.** (1987) 'Towards a unified analysis of gender and kinship' in Collier, J. and Yanigisako, S. (1987) editors, *Gender and Kinship: Essays Towards a Unified Analysis* Stanford: Stanford University Press.

YEATMAN, A. (1993) 'Voice and representation in the politics of difference' in **Gunew** and **Yeatman** (1993).

—— (1994) 'State and community', in Sharp, A. (1994) editor, *Leap into the Dark: the Role of the State in New Zealand* Auckland: Auckland University Press.

YOUNG, I. (1989) 'Polity and group difference: a critique of the ideal of universal citizenship' *Ethics* Vol. 99.

—— (1990a) 'The ideal of community and the politics of difference' in Nicholson, L. (1990a) editor, *Feminism/Post Modernism* New York and London: Routledge.

—— (1990) *Justice and the Politics of Difference* Princeton, NJ: Princeton University Press.

YUVAL-DAVIS, N. (1991) 'The citizenship debate: women, ethnic processes and the state' *Feminist Review* Vol. 39.

Reviews

Queer Looks: Perspectives on Lesbian and Gay Film and Video
Edited by Martha Gever, John Greyson and Pratibha Parmar
Routledge: London and New York, 1993
ISBN 0 415 90742 X, £15.99 Pbk

Daring to Dissent: Lesbian Culture from Margin to Mainstream
Edited by Liz Gibbs
Cassell: London and New York, 1994
ISBN 0 304 32796 4, £12.99 Pbk

The Good, the Bad and the Gorgeous: Popular Culture's Romance with Lesbianism
Edited by Diane Hamer and Belinda Budge
Pandora: London and San Francisco, 1994
ISBN 0 04 440910 9, £9.99 Pbk

FEMINIST REVIEW NO 51, AUTUMN 1995, pp. 113–152

It seems that pleasure and politics, when mixed together, can be strong stuff. That pleasure, alongside all those other aspects of the personal, is political is an established part of feminist thought. That politics can sometimes be pleasurable, not least for feminists, is a rather more controversial proposition. The question of how to strike a balance between the two is particularly urgent for feminists engaged in the field of cultural politics, and one which is variously addressed, directly and indirectly, by the essays in these three collections from the 'marginal' perspectives of lesbians and gay men.

The Good, the Bad and the Gorgeous sets out to examine what the subtitle calls 'popular culture's romance with lesbianism', otherwise known as 'lesbian chic': the recent and, to many lesbians, profoundly unsettling phenomenon of mainstream media fascination with (a glamorous version of) lesbianism, famously epitomized by the appearance of lesbian singer k d lang and is-she-or-isn't-she supermodel Cindy Crawford on the cover of the magazine *Vanity Fair*. Does 'lesbian chic' herald a new dawn of lesbian visibility – or is it just a shallow and probably short-term device for heterosexual consumers to pep up their tired old fantasy lives? The tension between visibility and commodification, and the fraught relationship between lesbianism and popular culture more generally, are explored in this collection in a variety of fields: popular music, print media, popular fiction, TV and cinema. Somewhat inevitably, perhaps, k d herself appears (sometimes with her supermodel companion) in the first five of these fifteen essays, beginning with the editors' introduction, and including Arlene Stein's excellent survey of the history of lesbians in popular music, from the 1970s to the present; Sonya Andermahr's intelligent critical interrogation of Madonna's 'truth or dare' lesbian image(s); and Sue O'Sullivan's analysis of the representation of lesbianism in the print media, which displays an admirable clear-sightedness about the vicissitudes of cultural politics.

Just over half the essays in the collection focus on the moving image – TV and cinema. The essays on TV assess the medium's various attempts to represent lesbianism: the highlight here for me was Margaret Marshment's and Julia Hallam's subtle, persuasive examination of the BBC adaptation of *Oranges are Not the Only Fruit*, which they regard as a successful translation of lesbian writing into 'mainstream' drama. The essays on cinema tackle the pleasure/politics problematic head on, perhaps because so much feminist film theory is still grappling with the legacy of Laura Mulvey's 1975 call to dismantle cinematic pleasure in the interests of feminist politics. Indeed, the impoverished state of current feminist film theory in matters of pleasure, particularly in relation to lesbians' pleasures as viewers of popular culture, is a recurrent topic in these essays, and a number of potential correctives are proposed, including Yvonne Tasker's reclamation of popular films often dismissed by feminist critics, and Paula Graham's complex and sophisticated approach to the question of the 'lesbian spectator' through a fascinating reading of the *Alien* trilogy. Interestingly, the essays on cinema are dominated by the film *Basic Instinct* almost as thoroughly as the essays on pop music and print media are dominated by k d lang – a point I'll return to shortly.

Like all collections, *The Good, the Bad and the Gorgeous* has some weak points: inevitably some essays are less successful than others, and writing on popular culture has its own dangers, not least the danger of writing as a fan instead of as a critic – Rosa Ainley's and Sarah Cooper's essay on country music comes perilously close to being just a list of favourite records – or, conversely, of merely denouncing pet hates rather than engaging with them. But the weak points are more than outweighed by the very considerable strengths of this collection, and I recommend it.

Daring to Dissent has a great deal of overlap with *The Good, the Bad and the Gorgeous* in its subject matter: it covers print media, popular fiction, TV, video and cinema, although it also includes essays on radio, theatre and poetry. There are some very good essays in this collection, and three in particular are excellent: Veronica Groocock's history of lesbian journalism, from *A3* in the 1960s to 'lipstick lesbians' in the glossies of the 1990s; Sheridan Nye's, Nicola Godwin's and Belinda Hollowes's survey of lesbians in radio, a rare example of this underrated medium being taken seriously as a potential route towards cultural empowerment; and Cherry Smyth's characteristically witty and confident discussion of recent lesbian film-making in the context of 'queer cinema'. On the whole, though, *Daring to Dissent* is less successful than *Gorgeous* as a collection, largely because it lacks the latter's clarity of intent: while *Gorgeous* concentrates on a particular cultural phenomenon, *Daring to Dissent*'s heterogeneity threatens to collapse into lack of focus, a threat which I find increased rather that otherwise by the division of its nine essays under five different subheadings. The collection also seems unsure of its audience; the editor's introduction appears to be pitched towards a *non*-academic readership, and as such is extremely readable, but I'm not sure how accessible that readership will find some of the essays, with references to Irigaray, Lacan, Judith Butler and the intricacies of feminist film theory.

It must also be said that, although there are a lot of good essays here, there are one or two distinctly bad ones. The coverage of TV compares particularly unfavourably with essays in *Gorgeous*: Rose Collis's shallow and dismissive attitude towards the TV dramas *Oranges are Not the Only Fruit* and *Portrait of a Marriage*, for example, is in sharp contrast to the intelligent discussion they each receive in *Gorgeous*. Moreover Collis's essay shares with some others in the collection a tendency towards an implausibly rigid dichotomy between 'lesbian culture' and 'mainstream culture', with lesbian culture posited as good (a 'wholesome validity', as one contributor puts it) and mainstream culture as bad. Feminist cultural politics cannot afford to ignore the fact that there are lesbians who do participate in, even gain pleasure from, 'mainstream' culture, with all its contradictions.

Both *The Good, the Bad and the Gorgeous* and *Daring to Dissent* present themselves as self-consciously lesbian enterprises: *Gorgeous* as a collection with, in the editors' words, a 'lesbian perspective', *Dissent* as an examination of, in the editor's words, 'lesbian genre'. This has a number of effects (not least of which, rather ironically, is their marketability:

lesbian chic is no stranger even to the world of feminist bookselling). The lesbian origins and focus are undoubtedly the driving force behind the collections themselves, giving them an impetus and a political edge that others may lack. They also act to foreclose certain lines of investigation, and these foreclosures are interesting in themselves – hence my intrigue at the recurrence of *Basic Instinct* in the pages of *Gorgeous*, where much of the critical attention and/or anxiety revolves around the question of whether the female protagonist, who engages in sexual behaviour with both women *and* men, is or is not lesbian. It's an interesting question – after all, what the hell *is* a lesbian anyway? – but a question which, precisely by virtue of their positioning as *lesbian* texts, the collections are unable to ask of themselves. It's symptomatic that bisexuality haunts both these collections like a troublesome ghost, regularly appearing in the guise of problem, unwanted 'negative image' ('switch-hitters', as Rose Collis puts it), or as simply disavowed (whole essays which discuss *Basic Instinct*, or Catherine Deneuve in *The Hunger*, and which don't even use the word 'bisexual'? Really?). This was a state of affairs I found troubling in the context of the alleged radicalness of the queer 1990s.

Queer Looks, a large and splendid volume on film and video, is, unlike the previous collections, a book by, and about the work of, both lesbians and gay men. The collection as a whole, perhaps inevitably, is dominated by the politics of HIV/AIDS, including discussions of AIDS activist video work, safer sex pornography, and cultural/political interventions against state homophobia and oppression of people living with HIV and AIDS. It firmly sets out, however, as the editors' introduction states, 'not to wallow in the grimness , but to fight back against it', and in this the book spectacularly succeeds: interesting, intelligent and politically engaged essays on film and video theory and practice, international cultural politics and political activism are interspersed with cartoons, interviews, personal reflections, photo-love stories and, for the artistically inclined, a make-your-own-lesbian-visibility-lampshade kit. The collection is divided into three parts: 'What a Difference a Gay Makes', on the current state of queer film and video; 'Favorite Aunts and Uncles', on heroes, heroines and pioneers; and 'Bedtime Stories', on contemporary representations of lesbian and gay sexuality. The work presented is of a consistently high quality and engages with its topics at all levels – film criticism, spectatorship theory, cultural history, practical film-making, funding, censorship, celebration. By turns funny, challenging, angry, moving and exhilarating, this book conveys a real sense of both pleasure *and* politics – the pleasure of politics, the politics of pleasure – without losing its grip on the seriousness of either. If you're remotely interested in lesbian and gay visual culture, you *must* get hold of a copy. That lampshade is just to die for.

Merl Storr

Bodies that Matter: On the Discursive Limits of 'Sex'
Judith Butler
Routledge: London, 1993
ISBN 0 415 90366 1 £10.99 Pbk, ISBN 0 415 90365 3 £35.00 Hbk

Outside in the Teaching Machine
Gayatri Chakravorty Spivak
Routledge: London, 1993
ISBN 0 413 90489 7, £12.99 Pbk, ISBN 0 415 90488 9, £35.00 Hbk

Postmodern Revisionings of the Political
Anna Yeatman
Routledge: London, 1994
ISBN 0 415 90198 7 £10.99 Pbk, ISBN 0 415 90197 9 £35.00 Hbk

Taken together, these three books may be said to reflect the various interpretative positions and political agendas currently defended within the spectrum of a poststructuralist feminism.

Yeatman is an avowed 'postmodernist' sociologist, who draws on her experience of the postcolonial situation in Australia and New Zealand to advocate a 'politics of representation' premised on the claim that there is no community of reason, because there is no collective, universal subject. Her book usefully serves to illustrate the terms of a 'postmodernist' political critique, but fails to address any of its more problematic aspects (save in the form of a brief discussion of a travestied version of Habermas). She has not decided whether postmodernist theory is telling us that representations constitute reality or that reality is only knowable via its representations; seems untroubled by the fact that the pluralism she advocates would imply giving equal respect to the experienced needs of both racist and anti-racist 'subjects'; and appears not to recognize that her attack on liberal humanism's imperialist conflations of cultural difference is motivated by a form of democratic 'reasoning' which can be justified only by reference to some minimal set of needs held in common across the human community.

Spivak's approach as a cultural critic working within the American academy from the optic of the outsider, is altogether more complex and canny. She, too, is concerned to explore the limits of any universalizing or generalist discourse, but her essays are marked throughout by her awareness of the potential political evasions of the anti-essentialist critique, and by her aspiration to some synthesis of deconstructivist and Marxist wisdoms. It remains deeply questionable how far these two can be forced into the political filiation she wants, but Spivak is a skilful matchmaker, whose deconstruction of the role of discourse in covering over the differences between specifically embodied and socially embedded individuals, notably those referred to through the generalizing categories of postcolonial theory (the 'Third World', the 'Asian', the 'subaltern' etc.), never loses sight of the fact that these differences are not to be theorized simply as the 'exclusions' of discourse, but are constituted through the structures of power of global capitalism. Spivak worries not only about the body as the site of gender inscription, but about the body in pain: the body exploited for its labour capacity, the body of the Indian bond-labour prostitute portrayed in Mahasweta Devi's novel, whose sexual 'identity' has never been at issue for her. She is an academic who questions – in highly theoretical ways – the legitimacy of theory as a form of politics, and is prepared to nag endlessly at the paradoxes of the deconstructive claim that the 'other' can only be represented in not being represented. In this collection you will find the usual ingredients of the Spivak essay: political acumen, arresting factual information and mind-numbing displays of theoretical reflexivity. If only Spivak could find a mode of expression which matched in its accessibility the wide-minded vision and democratic impulse of her message.

Butler's perspective is more circumscribed by her own identity as a North American lesbian intellectual keen to deploy deconstructive theory in the furtherance of a politics of sexual self-expression. In her new book she restates many of the themes of her earlier argument (the body is discursive construct: heterosexuality an imperative norm established through the abjection or exclusion of the lesbian body; sexual codes sustained only through reiterative performance) while seeking to clarify her position in the light of the charges of idealism and voluntarism laid against her earlier formulations. In 'concession' to her materialist critics, she now argues that 'construction' is not to be construed as 'artificial' or 'dispensable', but as 'constitutive constraint': as that 'without which we would not be able to think, to live, to make sense at all.' But since there are no bodies that are 'livable' and 'thinkable' other than as constrained by their material nature, this makes the terminology of 'construction' begin to seem purely prejudicial; and in asking us to view what is 'constructed' as indispensable, Butler is surely close to capsizing her fundamental project – which is to get us to see certain 'constitutive constraints', notably the living and thinking of the body as sexed, as merely normative and contingent.

Nor are things helped, it seems to me, by her further 'concessionary' claim that language and materiality are not opposed, since language 'both is and refers to that which is material and what is material never fully escapes the process by which it is signified'. For this clouds distinctions between the two orders which need to be observed. We may write the sign 'blood' in blood but the blood in which we write it no more affects the meaning of the term 'blood' than does using the term 'blood' in reference to blood alter the material composition of the latter.

Butler assumes that because we can only affirm a non-linguistic order linguistically, language is in some sense constitutive of the materiality affirmed. But to posit an extra-discursive materiality is to posit a reality which is not linguistic but subject to variable discursive representation. The real problem for any sexual or other form of politics is not the assertion of non-linguistic reality, but the assessment of the adequacy of the ways it is represented. To compromise on the recognition of reality in this sense is, paradoxically, to subvert the possibility of the political critique of any specific discourse upon it.

What Butler really needs is an ontological argument which enables her firmly to distinguish between what is and is not a culturally constituted constraint on the body, since without that she is at risk of reproducing all the worst offences of biologism in the form of cultural determinism. Indeed, when she goes on to argue that gender precedes subjectivity, and is prior to the emergence of the 'human', she appears to 'naturalize' gender in a way which is inconsistent with her (very cogent) critique of the Lacanian Symbolic (and of Žižek's deployment of Lacanian theory) for establishing an irrevocably phallic (hence masculinist) 'law' of sexual difference, while leaving it unclear what it is that established the gender matrix at all. If sex is the product of gender, what is gender: what distinguishes a *gender* performance or effect from any other performance or effect?

Butler's equivocation about the 'naturality' of the body is matched by equivocation in her use of the idea of the 'normative'. She offers powerful argument against any view of the convention or norm as deriving its authority from some pre-given Symbolic law, and argues that there is no 'law' of sexual identities and practices other than that enacted or spoken through reiterative performances. Performance is in obedience to convention, but convention is analysed as nothing but the aggregation of performances. But if the 'heterosexual' convention derives its social force only through a regular majoritarian practice then it is not clear what justifies its prescriptive presentation as a 'compulsion' rather than a 'preference'.

In terms of Butler's own analysis of a 'norm', there is no reason to suppose that heterosexuality is any less voluntary or pleasure-motivated than lesbianism, and her argument, in fact, trades on an untheorized asymmetry at this level whereby lesbian desire is allowed to figure in some obscure way as more spontaneous and 'authentic'. Butler, it is true, is reluctant to present lesbian desire as an excluded Truth, and tends to vacillate between a 'forbidden fruits' approach to its pleasure and desire and a less constructivist account of these, but if she is going to vacillate, she should vacillate equally in respect of heterosexuality. Either lesbian/gay sexual desire is brought into being only through its prohibition, in which case it, too, is experienced only in virtue of the 'norm', or it speaks to a 'natural' disposition which is different from the equally 'natural' and spontaneous disposition of heterosexuals. In short, it seems mistaken to suppose that defending lesbianism against its repudiation requires us to recognize the 'compulsory' nature of heterosexuality. All that is needed is to reject the cultural policing of same-sex relations as 'perverse' (a policing which many heterosexuals have always regarded as mistaken and do so today in increasing numbers).

This point has some bearing on her tendency to present same-sex relations as if they were 'unnameable' and 'unliveable' in our culture, which is surely to offer too demonic and essentialist a picture of heterosexual culture. It also relates to the paradoxical and double-edged nature of Butler's political agenda – which both wants to transform the Symbolic Order in ways which would make sexual orientation a matter of complete indifference (the direction in which, one might say, tolerance is always heading . . .) and at the same time to retain the lesbian or gay identity as that which is assumed and given political recognition only in and through its contestation with a hegemonic heterosexual Symbolic. To reveal the tensions within her position, however, is not to deny the interest and sophistication of her critical engagement with them in this wide-ranging collection of essays.

Kate Soper

Social Text 37 Winter 1993

Edited by Anne McClintock

Duke University Press/Durham NC

ISBN 0 74470 81235 7 $8.00, overseas add $2

Genders 19 November 1994
Sexual Artifice: Persons, Images, Politics

Edited by Ann Kibbey, Kayann Short and Abouali Farmanfarmaian

New York University Press

ISBN 0 8147 4651 9, $17.50 Pbk, ISBN 0 8147 4650 0, $50.00 Hbk

Social Text combines academic essays on the theme of the sex trade and sexuality with statements by sex workers and clients. While the political strategy of giving sex workers a space to speak for themselves – many complain of being spoken for while their own voices are silenced – is important, I did at first wonder how useful these accounts were. I am sure I am not alone in being fascinated to know what men will pay for and who does what in bed, but to some extent I feel 'so what?' Once you know that someone wants to be humiliated or to perform domestic labour with a cucumber up their bum, what difference does it make? Well, the main difference is that it challenges two prevalent myths that obscure debate and hinder policy about the sex trade. Firstly, prostitutes and other sex workers emerge as self-directing, articulate agents rather than as speechless victims; secondly, stereotypes about their clients and the services they offer are upturned – contrary to popular belief, the commercial SM scene is full of men who want to be dominated and the apparently small number of women who want a male dominator have problems finding one. In the first instance, the articles by sex workers indicate that many see their profession as a choice. While national and international organizations of prostitutes acknowledge the vagaries of the situation (and certainly never minimize the amount of coercion and violence in some regions or countries) women generally want prostitution to be seen as a job, with better pay and working conditions than other available employment. Most importantly, especially for anyone who wants to depict prostitutes as 'pure' in order to save them, it is clear that, like workers in any other field of employment, prostitutes are able to derive a sense of self-worth from a job well done and are proud of their skill and professional standing. The domina's emphasis on the skill involved in managing a bondage and discipline scene is not the false consciousness of a duped female, but the self-assessment of a worker practised in her field.

Sadomasochism and other forms of fetishism do occur often in this collection. Anne McClintock surveys a variety of such practices in the commercial sector (domestic 'slavery', bondage, babyism) and offers some useful speculations on what motivates their practitioners. She is helpfully clear on the differences between commercial consensual SM and common or garden sadism: SM is sex as consensual theatre involving 'social risk' which transforms pain into pleasure, dirt into value; sadism is non-consensual and has no sense of reversing social values (a man who beats his wife does not put on a rubber dress to do it). This piece, from which I learned much, is one of the few writings on SM that deals with the confused and often fragile boundary between consensual and non-consensual sexualized violence and that challenges the libertinism of the SM lobby. Troublingly, but intriguingly, this collection leaves me wondering whether the reason why only masochistic men are paying for services is because sadistic men can get/take what they want for free?

The new book-style version of *Genders* is concerned more broadly with the construction and representation of sexuality. Most of the articles in this issue are excellent and many are delightfully interdisciplinary. Rajeswari Mohan's impressive analysis of Indian cinema begins with the problem of authenticity raised by feminists speaking for/as/about Third World women and proceeds, via a discussion of the homogenization of women within contemporary Indian politics, to discuss how the female gaze in the films of K. Balanchander resitutes Western feminist film theory. The legacy of colonialism is further demonstrated by Heather Zwicker's discussion of the representation of gender in Northern Ireland. Her reading of Neil Jordan's *The Crying Game* shows how the film's ostensible revelation (that Dil has male genitalia) is less a problem of sex than of nation: 'if the individual human body [and its gendered identity] is almost infinitely permeable, how can the national body [and hence national identity] remain immutable?'. Similar, but less convincing, is Cynthia Weber's geopolitical analysis of male hysteria and the American invasion of Panama. Although I am quite taken with the picturing of Bush and Noriega as male hysterics, frantically overacting the phallic power they feel themselves to have lost, her tendency to indulge in word play results in specious observations – 'Furthermore, the name "Bush" announces the location of female genitalia' – that do not help her argument. Other articles, including those by Ian Barnard, Talia Schaffer, Leah Hackleman and Margaret A. Eisenhart and Nancy R. Lawrence demonstrate textual readings that address the role of fantasy in textual production and consumption and locate both in relation to material practice. Even when I am not entirely convinced by their conclusions, as in Barnard's analysis of Califia's *Macho Sluts*, I am inspired by the precision and thoughtfulness of their work. Eisenhart and

Lawrence, who address Anita Hill's perplexing loss of credibility during the Clarence Thomas hearing, are well worth a read and I was entranced by Schaffer's analysis of the photographs in *Orlando*. Her discussion of their relationship to the narrative (never straightforwardly illustrative, often oppositional) and the intimate family and friendship dynamics involved in their production, extends Butler's theory of performativity to challenge the potential normatization of masculinity: while the novel presents masculinity as a more 'natural', easily acquired state than femininity, the photographs reveal masculinity also to be a masquerade.

Reina Lewis

The Lesbian Postmodern
Edited by Laura Doan
Columbia University Press: New York, 1994
ISBN 0 231 08410 2, £42.50 Hbk

This collection of essays is curiously characterized by its contributors' musings about the point of it all. 'Why *lesbian postmodern*?' wonders Dana A. Heller (p. 173); 'when I was invited to submit an essay to this collection, my response was to disagree with the collection's premise', writes Judith Roof (p. 47). It is easy at first to endow the volume with a kind of fashionable postmodern superfluity. Why does everything have to be somehow brought into relation with postmodernism? And why a *lesbian*, rather than a gay, postmodernism? But it is the strength of this book to make you want to argue and to wonder why. A number of categories that have been vaguely dissolving around us are here vigorously and precisely contested: sexual essentialism, the commodification of lesbianism, the lesbian body, the relation between lesbianism and feminism. One of the conclusions of the book is that 'lesbian' as a category is irrelevant in a postmodern culture anyway: 'the end of lesbianism as we know it' (p. 99), and inevitably the dreaded p-word, 'postlesbian' (after postfeminism it was only a matter of time before her sister too was laid to rest).

Of course statements and arguments of this kind will irritate many. There is lived experience to reckon with, a category that even postmodernism has not quite managed to do away with. The everyday realities of 'living as a lesbian', for many women (and, according to this book, some who are not 'women'), repeatedly resist postmodernization in ways that make a lot of books, not only this one, feel faintly silly. This is of course part of a much wider discursive collision between theoretical writing and other, more pragmatic forms of cultural analysis and activism. But in the silliness there's still a kind of fascination and a strange kind of common sense. After reading *The Lesbian Postmodern* I really did feel that I had been forced to recognize that 'lesbian' was a category we could no longer take for granted, and that that shift was due only in part to the cultural phenomena that we tend to call 'queer'. In her introduction Robyn Wiegman powerfully sketches the extent to which the contemporary lesbian is defined by a 'commodity aesthetic' which allows us endlessly to buy into, and to consume, images of ourselves. She argues that postmodernism as a theory has the power to unsettle that short-circuit, to open up contradictions and mismatches in a 'different kind of encounter' (p. 16) which will re-invent both the 'lesbian' and the 'postmodern'. These are grand claims, but by the end I was convinced.

It was a clever move to place Sagri Dhairyam's 'Racing the lesbian, dodging white critics' first after the introduction. The implication of postmodernism in both constraining and progressive theories of race is an under-analysed area, but the racing of lesbianism is under-analysed in a different way. The paucity of theoretical material on lesbian as a white identity is well out of proportion to the activist energy devoted to the lives of non-white lesbians in both the US and here. Taking lesbian whiteness for granted is to our shame characteristic of the academy. As Dhairyam comments, 'the very bodies visible in academia are also produced by academic discourse as subject-effects of the professional discourses that empower their sub-jectivity' (p. 30), and those 'subject-effects' are white. Given that most readers of this book, which is more or less continuously academic in its style, will have some kind of academic background, it is chasteningly and creatively disorienting to find your own identity exactly and uncompro-misingly wrecked in its opening pages. Any flotsam you might have rescued will almost certainly be swept away by one of the later essays, perhaps Erica Rand's witty and provocative piece on Barbie dildos, Judith Halberstam's enquiry into the relation between transsexuals and lesbians, or Terry Brown's fascinating essay on the enigma of Jodie Foster.

But significantly essentialism is never simply discounted, and identity politics are continually worried at. Emma Pérez, in an essay on Chicana lesbians, describes herself as a 'strategic essentialist' (p. 105), and Cathy Griggers in a compelling essay on lesbians and postmodern technologies argues that we should not abandon, but 'refigure' our understanding of identity politics as 'a politics of transformation and hybridity as well as resistance' (p. 127). With 'identity' no longer what it was, 'identity politics' can no longer be what they once were. The unspoken imperative of the volume concerns the wider remit of politics in a postmodern era: where might they begin and end? Or are bodies, even lesbian ones, now only networks of organs and cyberspaces? If they are, maybe that is something to revel in. Elizabeth Grosz, in a poignant and inspiring piece on lesbian desire, suggests that we rethink desire beyond the paradigm of absence and lack into a new dynamic of energies, impulses and actions, 'the coming together of two surfaces' (p. 78). Perhaps this is where lesbian politics has gone in the 1990s, asking not 'am I – or are you – a lesbian but, rather, what kinds of lesbian connections, what kinds of lesbian-machine, we invest our time, energies and bodies in' (Grosz, p. 80).

Suzanne Raitt

Confronting Rape: The Feminist Anti-Rape Movement and the State
Nancy Matthews
Routledge: London and New York, 1994
ISBN 0 415 11401 2, £12.99 Pbk, ISBN 0 415 06491 0 £37.50 Hbk

This book traces the vicissitudes in rape crisis work in the US over two decades illustrating how the contradiction between the need for funding and the problems of collective leadership led to a move to professionalization and bureaucratization. Matthews argues that rape crisis in the US was influenced by a more conservative social services approach that threatened to submerge the more radical feminist political analysis regarding male violence, and shows how the state co-opted rape crisis and used it as a form of social control. She highlights the contradiction between providing an effective service for women through state funding in the context of a highly bureaucratized society and promoting an effective campaign to challenge male violence.

The contraction of social services under Reagan coincided with an increase in funding for victims of crime. From 1979 this was provided to the rape crisis groups studied here through the Californian Office of Criminal Justice Planning (OCJP). Support for rape crisis organizations was increasingly generous as long as they fitted into a mode of operation that was acceptable to the state. Many rape crisis centres had to rely on state funding in spite of their reservations about the compromises this involved and this inevitably led to a clash with feminist principles.

Very little has been written about rape crisis work as a social movement. The idealism and excitement of the early 1970s when left activists and members of the counter-culture were drawn into the rape crisis work, to share experiences and work as a collective, is vividly depicted. The roots of rape crisis work is traced to consciousness-raising groups where validating women's experiences was seen as leading to direct action for social change. Great importance was placed on empowering women who had been raped by encouraging them to make their own decisions. Central to the position of many of these groups was a political aim to transform the relations between men and women, and shift the responsibility for violence from women to men and make visible those responsible for assaults. Matthews describes some brave attempts to confront rapists or take direct action against them, an approach far removed from the legal bureaucratic system of redress and one which was stopped in its tracks by men suing the groups for slander.

The exhilaration of consciousness raising and collective action is vividly described along with the conflicts and crises of the work of six rape crisis centres in Los Angeles. The real conflict between resisting hierarchical managerial forms and dependence on state funding and keeping the service together so as to provide an effective counselling service is vividly spelt out. Matthews integrates an understanding of the ways in which difference between women from different cultural contexts affected their orientation to rape. The need to preserve family life led the Chicanas to press for including men, African American women saw rape in the context of the historical connexion between rape, racism and lynching, whereas Asian women stressed the importance of privacy and the needs of immigrant women. For women of colour rape crisis work was often a career rather than a voluntary activity as it was for white women, which often led them to be more conciliatory towards working within the state.

This book has implications for understanding the dynamics of the way social movements are transformed through their relations with the state. The radicalism of a vital campaign for women's liberation developed into an accepted part of service provision. This involved the adoption of a more formalized structure and a focus on direct service provision rather than direct political action and a far more bureaucratized, hierarchical system of management. This resulted in the depoliticization of rape in the sense that the feminist analysis of gendered power relations was removed from the picture. Matthews pessimistically argues that although this was done under the humanistic mantle of providing services for traumatized women, it also involved co-option of the movement. More positively, she adds that women working in state agencies still attempted covertly to resist bureaucratic requirements and that real political successes could be claimed for the redefinition of rape as violence rather than sexual, and for the critique of the judicial system.

In Britain where rape crisis workers have resisted state control to a greater extent than in the US, often to the detriment of their funding, similar contradictions have arisen. Here too state funding has been shifted to supporting the more politically palatable victim support services and therapeutic initiatives, leaving rape crisis centres severely underresourced and able to provide only a skeleton service. Yet as Matthews shows, accepting state funding inevitably leads to a more accommodating stance. Within this context this book is invaluable in identifying the possibilities of working with the state without 'selling out' or retreating into separatism. It does, however, underline the real conflicts and contradictions that arise both in relation to the focus of the work and the structure of the organization and process of decision-making. In practice, Matthews argues, bureaucracy is necessary in a society where it is so pervasive and where it gave the movement access to resources without which it could no longer function.

Sue Lees

The Usurer's Daughter: Male Friendship and Fictions of Women in Sixteenth-century England

Lorna Hutson
Routledge: London, 1994
ISBN 0 415 05049 9 £40.00 Hbk

You can choose your friends, but you can't choose your relations: from a historical perspective, this apparently obvious distinction looks less certain. Until around the seventeenth century 'friends' meant those close to you, whether kin or not, so the contrast drawn in the proverb would be meaningless. Moreover, the notion that friends might be primarily people you *chose*, motivated by a sense of sympathy and common principles, rather than those attached to you by codes of tradition and loyalty, is equally historical; and the sixteenth century in England is a period of transition in this as in so much else. The meaning of friendship, specifically of friendship between men, mutates away from the alliances of a quasi-feudal and militarized nobility, held in place by codes of honour and the exchange of gifts, towards the insecure and speculative alliances of a mobile and educated courtly culture, characterized as freely chosen bonds between like-minded men. Throughout the sixteenth century a stream of literature comments on and participates in this shift, reflecting directly or indirectly on the nature, duties and pleasures of friendship, evoking it as an idealized guiding principle, a solace in a harsh and untrustworthy world. The pleasure which the literature insists on is that of the meeting of minds. Sympathy in the fullest sense is identified as the privilege of friendship.

This process of transformation and redefinition is the starting point for Lorna Hutson's wide-ranging and impressive analysis, which engages both with the nature of the humanist reinvention of friendship, and with its consequences for the representation of women in the literature of the period. Her argument moves persuasively across disciplinary boundaries, drawing on economics and anthropology alongside history and literature, investigating legal, religious and didactic writings as well as fiction and drama, encompassing along the way topics such as housekeeping, female chastity and theories of comedy, in addition to her primary subject matter of male friendship. All are drawn together into an account which places women crucially as signs of love and friendship between men, in an extended contest over the nature of masculinity.

This transformation, inevitably, was productive of anxiety; where friendship had once been guaranteed in the definite symbols of the vow and the gift, humanism had a destabilizing impact. On the one hand it scorned and devalued the concrete symbol, regarding the exchange of gifts as unworthy of the educated man, whose love should be guided by sympathy, not by inducement. But at the same time, by displacing the signs of true friendship into speech acts, the humanists gave rise to a whole new set of problems; for the speech act, which was valued the more the greater its rhetorical skill, was also undermined by the uncertainty at the heart of persuasive rhetoric: how can one know whether the words spoken are purely for effect? How is persuasive skill to be distinguished from deceit? For, of course, the high-minded account of friendship as meeting of minds is only part of the story. Friends remained people who did things for you, who had your interests at heart and cared for your credit; and friends might advantageously be won on false pretences. The instability in concepts such as 'interest' and 'credit', crossing the boundaries between economics and personal honour, is not a matter of chance; and women as signs of credit between men are similarly positioned.

Simultaneously, masculinity itself was in the process of redefinition – 'From Errant Knight to Prudent Captain', as Hutson puts it. Humanist writings on domestic economy elaborate a version of the ideal household founded on the contrast and separation of men's and women's activities, governed (of course) by the prudent man. These functioned, Hutson argues, as an intervention into the contemporary debates on economics in the marketplace, and the whole embittered question of the charging of interest – usury – by way of a notion of the good ordering and use of worldly goods. The need to train a wife in such right use and order serves to justify carefulness: 'the Christian layman is able to transgress the permitted bounds of his worldly activities to the extent that such transgression redefines him as a good husband' (p. 49). The idea of the well-taught and well-governed wife, who looks after her husband's interests, further extends into the sexual sphere: she will conserve his honour and use her value with care, just as she would not waste any other of his goods.

But if the household could thus become the defining space for the relation between the careful wife and her enterprising husband, it was also a space which might be entered and violated under the sign of friendship. Implicit in the system is the possibility of betrayal, not only by the wife, but by the friends who may after all be dangerous. It is this possibility that Hutson sees at work in the stories of the mid sixteenth century which she discusses in the middle part of the book, which she describes as 'a literature featuring men who seem obsessed with the problem of "reading" the probable signs of clandestine sexual activity between their wives and daughters and the male "friends" to whom they risk having given the persuasive edge by having (in friendship) communicated too much' (p. 85). These stories she candidly acknowledges are generally now seen as unreadable, and her success in making them seem readable, or at least comprehensible, is one of the most interesting aspects of the book. It is, she argues, precisely because these tales are attempting to redefine masculinity as persuasion rather than force that the story takes second place to the debates: 'fiction ceases to be solely concerned with feats of chivalry, and begins to incorporate the endless reasoning *pro et contra* of which modern readers despair' (p. 97). Real men, in the humanist version of manhood, don't fight; they make plans, and argue.

The uncertainty about meaning which the process of argument around doubtful possibilities implies is both disturbing and productive for the writer. The last section of the book examines this uncertainty in relation to two of Shakespeare's comedies, *The Comedy of Errors* and *The Taming of the Shrew*, following up Hutson's opening proposition that 'there is a very precise correlation between the centrality of women to the fiction and drama of the English Renaissance, and the extent to which that fiction and drama acknowledged its own problematic implication in the highly productive but radically uncertain mediation of friendships resting "wholly in a meeting of minds"' (pp. 8–9). It is, she argues, 'the audience's uncertainty about their sexual intentions and desires' (p. 190) that marks a radical break between the women of Shakespeare's drama and that of the earlier parts of the century, in which women figure as almost invariably already unchaste, fixed in their dramatic function of setting young men against their fathers. Once again, too, the 'persuasive fiction' addressed to women in a specifically humanist sense offers to fashion them, to mould them textually, and thereby justifies the apparent immorality of the theatre: it cannot be immoral if it persuades women that chastity is good.

This discussion perhaps shows symptoms of researcher's tunnel vision, the condition in which one's chosen subject of research is found in and comes to explain everything in the world: it is difficult to feel that humanist theories of argument and plausibility, however influential, entirely account for the representation of women in a form so rich and diverse as Elizabethan and Jacobean drama. Similarly, at the outset Hutson declares that her reading of the representation of women excludes 'contemporary discourses of sexuality and the psyche' in favour of 'a sixteenth-century socio-economic discourse of friendship', but in fiction and drama that at least appears to be concerned very directly with questions of desire and sexuality, it seems a very large exclusion. To read that the story of the Countess of Celant, a narrative of marriage, several love affairs and murder, 'is not, after all, anything to do with female sexuality', is disconcerting; it is easy enough to accept that it is to do with *more* than that, that female sexuality on its own is too readily taken as a catch-all explanation without regard to historical and cultural change; but surely a reading through contemporary (and sixteenth-century) concerns about sexuality and the psyche may also be productive, though differently. Despite its wide disciplinary range, too, the book's focus can seem unduly limited. Is the process being described specific to England, or part of a more general European humanist enterprise, and if the latter, what are the implications of this for the more culturally specific parts of the argument? Does the omission of poetry from the discussion mark a significant difference, or simply lack of space?

Overall, however, this is a very impressive and interesting book, in both its conceptual scope and its scholarship. It makes some demands on the reader, it is clearly aimed at a specialist readership, able to handle the procession of obscure names and rhetorical concepts. But it is thought-provoking and original work, giving insight into unfamiliar material, and new perspectives on the familiar.

Kate Hodgkin

Servicing the Middle Classes
Nicky Gregson and Michelle Lowe
Routledge: London, 1994
ISBN 0 415 08531 4, £13.99 Pbk, ISBN 0 415 08530 6, £40.00 Hbk

This is an important book dealing with a topic which sits squarely at the intersection of 'private problems with public issues'. It is the first serious academic study of the return of domestic servants in the 1970s and 1980s – something that surely we all knew about, but which nobody has systematically studied until now.

The book combines geographical with sociological perspectives and is divided into two parts. The first looks at the temporal and spatial trends in the distribution of domestic servants during the 1980s and at the determinants of 'demand' (why people want to employ them) and 'supply' (why people want these jobs). Demand is explored in two ways. First by analysing advertisements for domestic servants of various kinds in *The Lady* magazine, a national publication, and in local newspapers covering the two local labour markets studied: Newcastle and Reading, between July 1981 and June 1991. Those aspects of family relationships and interactions which influence whether couples will employ domestic servants are explored in interviews with 300 households in Reading and Newcastle with both partners in full-time professional or managerial employment. This reveals that couples who share domestic tasks fully are far less likely than those with a more traditional division of labour to employ servants (32% versus 85%).

Thirty-two per cent of even those with fully shared domestic labour is still a high proportion, and Gregson and Lowe go on to a more theoretical discussion of why it is that the use of servants by even these families is now so widespread. In their attempt to unpack (as they put it) this aspect of the demand for paid domestic labour, the authors range widely over sociological ideas about leisure. Although this is a valuable and necessary beginning to such discussion, it is perhaps slightly less successful than some other parts of the book. The authors have not quite made contact with the notion of leisure activity as a source of 'Distinction'. I believe Bourdieu shows us that what is done in leisure time and thereby made available for display to others is itself a part of the constant struggle to gain and maintain status. By failing to explore this aspect of what constitutes 'quality' leisure time, the book misses one part of the puzzle. Low status activity takes up time which striving middle-class couples feel they would be better advised to spend doing things which either bring them more into contact with higher status or more powerful reference groups, or provide

FEMINIST REVIEW NO 50, SUMMER 1995

creditable and status-enhancing topics for discussion with significant others. In the heightened status-struggles of the 1980s and 1990s such considerations probably strengthened.

Such a perspective would also help to solve a question not raised at all in the book but which leapt out from the excellent interview material: why do some of these people, with the attitudes they expressed (especially some of the fathers), wish to have children at all? One reason is that being able to display the existence of a family is creditable and status-enhancing in our present society. In the same way, feminist sociologists of organization have shown, the trick is to get someone else in the office to do the hard work, and keep the appearance of skill, competence (virility? femininity?) etc. for oneself. Men have traditionally done this to women. Now we are seeing what happens when middle-class women start doing it to working-class women. Gregson and Lowe return in the final chapter to the social and political implications of this. This discussion is rather taciturn, but who is to blame them? The whole topic is so emotionally charged, and the book maintains an almost frustratingly cool stance throughout: only in the acknowledgements do we find heartfelt declaration that 'this book was written without the assistance of any waged domestic labour'!

The question of 'supply', and the more complex aspects of the relationships between employers and employees, is investigated by in-depth interviews with 30–40 employees and 15 'employer/servant pairs' in each of the two study areas. The increase in the supply of women willing to take on other people's domestic work for low wages is elegantly explained in terms of two main trends. The number of young women with some nursery training willing to work in private households is influenced by the falling numbers of childcare jobs in publicly provided institutions such as hospitals and council nurseries. The increased supply of cleaners is due to increased un- and non-employment and the reduction in benefit levels which means that more women now live on benefits of one kind or another, and must take additional jobs to make ends meet. None of the cleaners (and only some of the nannies) was employed 'on the books'.

The authors themselves seem not fully satisfied with their own explanation of why some young women become private nannies. They found that these women came from traditional families and were taking stopgap work until they themselves could marry and set up similar households. There is almost a critical stance towards their 'traditionalism'. And yet if all men and women were highly qualified and did interesting paid work, someone would still have to look after children. Why do we not place more value on the desire to care, and give this option higher priority in political demands? The vivid interview material leaves one feeling that many of the middle-class children were extremely lucky to have carers who did not resent time spent with them as their parents seemed to. Some nannies became deeply attached to their young charges despite the fact that these children would not represent a source of status to them, either in the present or even less in the future (who will be invited to degree ceremonies and christenings, or qualify for support in old age?). Surely this commitment must be something to value? And then there is the other side of the coin: surely there needs to be some questioning of what pressures adults still feel to produce children even though they have little desire to care for them?

The fact that this book arouses so sharply these very painful questions and allows one to begin to think 'theoretically and politically' about them is perhaps the greatest of its many qualities. It is not beginners' reading, but should be obligatory for all second-year and above students in sociology and social policy and their teachers, and highly recommended for all the social sciences (including economics and psychology).

Mel Bartley

Feminism and Geography
Gillian Rose
Polity Press: Cambridge, 1993
ISBN 0 7456 1156 7, £11.95 Pbk, ISBN 0 7456 0818 3, £39.50 Hbk

Feminism has made its presence felt in the discipline of geography for some two decades. Since the early 1970s feminists working in human geography have sought to expose, challenge and overcome the various ways in which women are ignored, misrepresented and mistreated in the discipline. This project has entailed developing strategies to secure gender equality at all levels within the discipline; it has entailed critiquing the body of knowledge called geography; it has entailed attempting to create a new kind of geography.

Gillian Rose's book, *Feminism and Geography*, is an important and original contribution to this project. She draws on a body of feminist theory to elaborate her claim that 'to think geography – to think within the parameters of the discipline in order to create geographical knowledge acceptable to the discipline – is to occupy a masculine subject position' (p. 4). And she explores how feminists might think differently in order to resist and go beyond the masculinism of geography.

Rose's critique of geographical knowledge is powerful and far-reaching. She draws on feminist analyses of rational knowledge to argue that geography, like other disciplines, is underpinned by an intrinsically masculine position that nevertheless claims to be universal. From this basis she elaborates some of the particular ways in which masculinity defines geography. She distinguishes between a 'social-scientific masculinity', which 'asserts its authority by claiming access to a transparently real geographical world', and an 'aesthetic masculinity', which 'establishes its power through claiming a heightened sensitivity to human experience' (pp. 10-11). To illustrate the operation of these versions of masculinity she takes as examples approaches in geography that are in some ways rather attractive for feminist researchers.

Rose's first example is time-geography, which entails tracing everyday lives through time and space in order to understand social life in its spatial context. The emphasis on routine and ordinary behaviour holds obvious attractions for feminist geographers. However, Rose shows how time-geography assumes 'that space can always be known and mapped'; that space is 'absolutely knowable' (p. 38). This 'claim to see all and know all' (p. 39) implicitly erases what is specific about the one who claims to know. In so doing it entails assuming a masculine subject position, which she describes as 'social-scientific'. Rose argues that this masculinism explains why attempts by feminist geographers to use time-geography to examine women's lives have found the framework unable to capture vital dimensions of everyday life, namely 'the emotional, the passionate, the disruptive, and the feelings of relations with others' (p. 28).

Rose illustrates the operation of 'aesthetic masculinity' through a very different strand of geographical research, namely that concerned with the human experience of place. This too holds out attractions for feminist geographers because of the way it appears to validate experiential knowledge. But Rose shows how this tradition relies upon a concept of place that is implicitly feminine. Consequently, it refers only to the experience associated with a masculine subject position.

If geographical knowledge is *intrinsically* masculine, feminist geography becomes a contradiction in terms. But rather than give up on geography altogether, Rose defines the task of constructing a new kind of geography in a manner that makes it possible to draw creatively on contradictoriness. She argues that feminists necessarily adopt an ambivalent position both in and against the discipline of geography. And she advocates a strategy that makes use of other kinds of ambivalence as well. She draws on the writings of Teresa de Lauretis to argue for a 'critical mobility' that allows feminists to destabilize and disrupt the certainties associated with the existing parameters of geographical knowledge by, as it were, operating on more than one front.

Studies of the material conditions of women's lives provide an example of this kind of oscillation. Rose interprets such work as 'an ambivalent discourse straddling the need to represent women and the need to speak of differences among women' (p. 116). There are risks associated with this in that it is easy to slip from ambivalence into the dichotomous structure that characterizes hegemonic systems of knowledge. Rose suggests that this is apparent in a tendency to emphasize similarities among women in terms of their domestic and family lives, and differences among women in terms of their involvement in paid work, a contrast complicit with masculinist dichotomies such as private and public, home and work. And this tendency provides an explanation for the difficulty feminist geographers have experienced in addressing issues of racism and sexuality. But Rose suggests that there are possibilities for escaping this kind of dichotomy by consciously oscillating 'between the elaboration of diversity and the solidarity of sisterhood' (p. 132). This allows feminist geographers to insist on the inappropriateness of such dichotomous categories as private and public, and to open up new spaces that are 'neither the masculine public nor the femininized private' (p. 136).

Feminism and Geography provides those working within the discipline of geography with a distinctive reading of the project of feminist geography as it has developed to date, and some ideas about future directions. For those unfamiliar with the discipline it brings some of the issues specific to geography into relation with broader debates within feminism. It is very much an academic book (and Rose acknowledges her own complicity with the masculinist traditions of academic knowledge), but this does not detract from its value as an introduction to the field of feminist geography. I hope it encourages readers of *Feminist Review* to discover more of the contribution to women's studies that emanates from this quarter.

Liz Bondi

Our Sister's Land

Edited by Jane Aaron, Teresa Rees, Sandra Betts and Moira Vincentelli
University of Wales Press: Cardiff, 1994
ISBN 0 7083 1247 0, £12.95 Pbk

It is astonishing how little has been written on women's lives in Wales, a quarter of a century after the women's movement began to affect all our lives. Resources of any kind are still scarce, so this book deserves a warm welcome in helping to plug a very large gap. Having decided to produce a book in English, the editors can hope not only to serve the needs of the increasing number of students, many of them non-Welsh-speaking, taking courses in women's studies in Wales, but also to raise the consciousness of inmigrating women and women in other parts of Britain, who tend to be largely unaware of the particular experiences of Welsh women, or make assumptions based on clichéd images.

The fact that so little published material is available in this field has led the editors to include a variety of material, in order to present 'the diversity of current Welsh women's experience'. Thus the volume is divided into two parts, the first containing essays of a sociological nature, investigating women's lives in the home and the community on the one hand, and in the public spheres of education, training and work on the other. The second section includes both academic-type essays on culture and politics as well as a series of seven personal accounts by women in diverse walks of life, including writers, an artist, a businesswoman, an Anglican deacon and a Welsh-language activist. Although the broad scope of the volume makes it an ideal starting point for the uninitiated, it lacks unity, reminding me forcibly of very early collections of feminist writing, such as *Conditions of Illusion* (Feminist Books, 1974). Have we progressed so little in twenty years?

For many readers the chapters may seem tantalizingly, even frustratingly short, especially those in the form of academic essays. Some of the latter are staggeringly superficial, their conclusions banal, and I was disturbed by the lack of scholarly rigour in the first section. Where conclusions are based on interviews of samples, we are not always told how large the sample was, how the interviewees were chosen, and what was their socio-economic status. It is not always clear, either, in what language they were interviewed: it does make a great difference. Coming from a Welsh-speaking rural community, I found it incredible that the essay on 'Old women in rural Wales' casually mentioned that some of the women interviewed were Welsh-speakers without considering the commonplace problem of language-shift in two and three generations of the family: the language adopted by their children and grandchildren is of central significance to many older women, a source of joy or of distress and alienation. The language of their neighbours is similarly crucial.

None the less, a useful collection of data and statistics emerges from this section, especially with regard to employment, where women are clearly worse off than their English sisters, earning a smaller proportion of the male average wage, and even more under-represented in the professions and in business. I should have liked more discussion of why this should be so, linked perhaps to the wider question of Welsh identity.

As Welsh-speakers, we can define ourselves by our separate language and our acceptance or refusal of the traditional cultural structures with which it has historically been associated. But with only a fifth of the population speaking the language, it is necessary to consider in what way the other four-fifths have any separate identity from women in, say, England. A number of the sociological essays – on attitudes to housework, on experiences of mature students, for example – would easily be applicable in an English context, and in general both editors and contributors to this section have failed to consider why there is a need to treat Wales separately. If women in Wales *are* different and have different experiences because they live in Wales, even if they belong to the thousands of recent in-migrants from England, then the book is justified, but one could be forgiven for concluding, after reading those essays, that all we have in common is a geographical space. The photographs do not help in this respect, for few reflect specifically Welsh experience. Furthermore, they are both dated and over-familiar within Wales.

Although the book provides a very fair balance between north and south, some of the generalizations are disturbing, for example the assumption that the clichéd image of the 'Welsh mam' has been consistent within Wales as a whole. This is simply not true: it has grown up mainly in the industrial areas of the south where men's wages in coal and steel, for example, were considered as 'family wages'. In the rural and semi-industrial areas of mid-Wales and the north, where male wages were lower, women normally engaged in agricultural or other productive work, thus making a significant contribution to the family economy (as they still do, as Shan Ashton's pioneering article on farm women shows), so that the image of the stay-at-home wife and mother was far less prevalent.

Those who really want to learn more about our lives this side of the border and what it *feels* like to live in Wales, should concentrate on the second section. Here the largely descriptive essays of the first section give way to greater analysis, and in many instances a stronger political framework. Jane Aaron's introductory essay on 'Gender and colonization' provides a clear and fair overview for English readers, although she has not managed to capture the appropriate linguistic register in translating from the work of Angharad Tomos. Gwyneth Roberts's analysis of Raymond Williams's portrayal of women in his novels looks at first somewhat out of place, but, given that Williams's thought is still influential in many quarters in Wales and beyond, it provides a necessary warning that his vision of an ideal society is essentially man-centred. The personal accounts are full of treasures: Angharad Tomos's moving account of women involved in the language movement, a brave, hidden sisterhood unguessed at by English feminists; Roni Crwydren's struggle to define herself personally, politically

FEMINIST REVIEW NO 50, SUMMER 1995

and culturally as a lesbian on the fringes of the Welsh-speaking community; Mary Lloyd Jones's analysis of her life as an artist, full of telling detail as she gradually locates herself as an artist and Welsh-speaking woman, weaving the political and the lyrical, anger and hope; Menna Elfyn showing that it is possible to be Welsh activist, poet and feminist at the same time. The book would be worth reading for these alone. For those who think of Wales in terms of the Wales Tourist Board's images of mountains, castles, tall hats and harps, *Our Sister's Land* will provide a valuable corrective, and even some shocks.

Ceridwen Lloyd-Morgan

Western Women and Imperialism: Complicity and Resistance
Edited by Nupur Chaudhuri and Margaret Strobel
Indiana University Press: Bloomington and Indianapolis, 1992
ISBN 0 253 20705 3 Pbk, ISBN 0 253 31341 4 Hbk

As the editors of this collection are all too well aware, all histories of imperialism necessarily tread a fine line between unmasking the violence of the colonial encounter and capitalizing on the all too prevalent nostalgia for a mythic moment where men were 'men' and women were 'ladies'. In this scenario European women exist primarily as the passive beneficiaries of an ancient chivalric code – living out a stable class existence in exotic locations unthreatened by the disruptions accompanying the growth of industrial capitalism in the metropolitan centres of empire. The indigenous populations exist solely as foils for the main movers in the narratives of imperial melodrama who are almost uniquely the masculine heroes of *Boys Own* fame, battling against recalcitrant 'native' insurgents or policy-making from the comfort of overstuffed leather in the seclusion of the 'club'.

Chaudhuri and Strobel's collection succeeds in disrupting this fantasy and in reinstating the central role of women in the propagation of imperial ideology. The essays in this collection go much further than this however. Recognizing the way in which such a strategy of recovery risks supplanting one set of 'heroes' with another equally dubious set of 'heroines', neither of which dislodges the main tenets of the colonial imaginary, the editors have been careful to select a series of contributions which demonstrate the ways in which gender intersected with class and 'race' in complex and contradictory ways at various moments in the history of Western imperialism. *Western Women and Imperialism* is a rich and accessible introduction to a wide range of issues and problems associated with the historiography of the colonial encounter and the heterogeneity of women's experiences as participants in the colonial project. Any criticism of the collection can perhaps be confined to a concern over the almost exclusive concentration on middle-class women's involvement in and experience of colonialism and a lack of consideration over the impact which imperialism made on the lives of lower middle-class and working-class women in Britain, North America and the colonies. Despite the broader historical span signalled in many of the titles, the majority of the contributions focuses on the nineteenth and early twentieth centuries. This leaves Karen Tranberg Hansen's important article on the impact of class relations for the development of racism in post-World-War-II Northern Rhodesia somewhat out on a limb at the end of the collection. In addition, any collection which focuses primarily on British imperialism, as this one does, should include some contribution to the long-standing intersections of class and gender in the history of British imperialism in Ireland.

While one of the strengths of these essays is the extent to which many of them engage on some level with the impact of colonial intervention on the lives of the indigenous populations, the focus of the collection is on white Western women's participation in India and Africa. It is an emphasis which serves as a timely reminder, as Leslie Fleming points out in her essay on American missionaries' ideals for North Indian women, of the need for further research exploring Indian and African women's responses to such initiatives in order fully to appreciate the dynamics of the colonial encounter as a two-way process (p. 204). Two essays do engage with this important issue. Mervat Hatem's contribution is the only one to foreground the dialectical relation between European women's orientalist writings and the emergence of an Egyptian nationalist literature produced by Egyptian and Levantine-Egyptian women. In a carefully historicized account of the dissemination and production of these texts between 1862 and 1920 she analyses the ways in which, despite disparities in the power relations of one to the other, both were produced through and mobilized myths about each other's status and lived experiences. Mrinalini Sinha unmasks the centrality of gender in the debates over the Ilbert Bill (1883–1884) and the involvement of the native women of the Bengali *bhadramahila* in the fight to remove the discriminatory clause from the Indian Penal Code which banned Indian civil servants from exercising criminal jurisdiction over European British subjects living outside the chief Presidency towns. Sylvia Jacobs provides a tantalizing segment of her research on the impact of the triple inscription of race, gender and imperialism on the experience of Black women missionaries from North America.

If there is a leitmotif in the group of essays presented in this collection it is as Callaway and Helly state in their conclusion, that simply to dismiss any of the European women analysed in the book 'as racists and participants in contemporary imperialism without understanding their personal experiences and springs of motivation, their complexities and ambiguities, leaves us with labels, not history' (p. 94). Their answer is to explore the life and writings of such women as Flora Shaw (later Lady Lugard and colonial correspondent for *The Times* between 1890 and 1900) within the context and constraints of their own lived experience in order to gain 'a more textured understanding of gender, ideology and imperialism' (p. 94). In recent years much important work has set about deconstructing the central tropes of colonial discourse. This group of essays can perhaps be appreciated as a complementary intellectual project, producing another much needed materialist account which retrieves the historical specificity of the diversity of political and economic conditions underlying the colonial encounter and the possibilities and limitations of the kinds of intervention available to white middle-class women in Britain and (to a lesser extent) in North America. To this end many of the essays address the ambivalent nature of the power ascribed to Western women in their role as guardians of the imperial 'race' and the ways in which this circumscribed their own definitions of 'femininity' and female sexuality. Dea Birkett's essay on the Colonial Nursing Association (founded in 1896) focuses on the tension between the concept of nursing as a vocation staffed by women conforming to the ideal of the Victorian 'lady', whose primary role was conceived as guardian of those moral values associated with the imperial 'race', and the conflicting desire of many nurses themselves for public recognition of their labour as a demanding and highly skilled profession. Nancy Paxton explores the way in which the prevailing Victorian ideology of all women's sexuality as highly dangerous and potentially destabilizing ultimately informs the politics and actions of women as politically opposed as anti-suffragist Flora Annie Steel and the socialist Annie Besant.

Crucially, the ways in which the histories of even liberal and radical Western feminism are implicated in imperial ideology does not escape scrutiny in the collection. Antoinette Burton's exemplary contribution analyses the reasons why many middle-class women and feminists in nineteenth-century Britain bought into their imperialist identification as moral redeemers and were able to capitalize on this as a way of strengthening their own indispensability to the state. Burton teases out the contradictions of liberal feminist discourse and its dependence on tenets of empire and Christian evangelism. The essay begins with an analysis of the implications for Indian and European women once Josephine Butler's crusade against the Contagious Diseases Act was transferred from the British to the Indian context. Burton then moves to an exploration of feminist writings on Indian women in British women's periodicals of the period. Here she convincingly maps the extent of the imperialist assumptions underlying the desire for a universal womanhood which, while aiming to 'transcend [ ] national and racial boundaries', often relied on casting the Indian woman as a voiceless victim of her own society in need of the protective care of her benevolent and 'wiser' Western sisters (p. 148). Sinha's essay raises the same problem when she analyses the contradictions inherent in the liberal Annette Ackroyd's attack on the Ilbert Bill in 1883 (p. 110).

Many of the essays also serve to highlight the difficulties of doing this kind of historical research. Scant documentation on women's participation in many of the central institutions of Western imperialism necessitates inventive research methods and reminds us of the need not only to constitute the archive but to question the nature of the existing archive as a source for historical investigation. Such research also emphasizes the interdisciplinary nature of almost all feminist histories and our own imperative to incorporate the insights provided by oral histories, anthropology, literary theory and sociology while respecting the precepts of distinct disciplinary procedures.

Notwithstanding the paternalistic agenda clearly underwriting missionary, nursing and other colonial endeavours, the essays in this collection hint at another important outcome of the colonial encounter and one which has significant implications for continuing research. As Jacobs and Fleming both point out, the fundamental changes to the social and economic structure of African and Indian women's lives, through education, literacy, health care and contraception, while stemming from a total disregard for the significance and value of any indigenous institutions, were often productive of other skills and desires which in some instances contributed to the breakdown of the very imperial order which the colonial emissaries sought to implant in their 'charges'. In other words, what some of this research provides is a glimpse of the fact that the colonial subject was neither as obedient nor as contained as some of the more monolithic histories of imperialism would have us believe.

Annie E. Coombes

The Color of Gender: Reimagining Democracy

Zillah R Eisenstein

Berkeley: University of California Press, 1994

ISBN 0 520 08422 5, $15.00 Pbk, ISBN 0 520 08422 5, $45,00 Hbk

As a feminist, Zillah Eisenstein begins by locating this book within her own personal and political context. The acknowledgements include her daughter's teachers and other carers who enabled Zillah Eisenstein to have the time and energy to write, and the introductory chapter starts with the political influences on a child of communist parents in the USA of the 1950s. Eisenstein wants to re-imagine democracy 'between the legacy of the Reagan–Bush decade and the possibility of change' that appears to be offered by Hillary and Bill Clinton. Writing as a white woman in a society based on 'a racialized system of difference threaded through with economic class and gender privilege' which she terms racialized patriarchy, Zillah Eisenstein argues that 'difference' implies power and oppressive structures more than diversity. *The Color of Gender* does not focus on the texts of white men, which is a refreshing change for a feminist text in the wake of Foucault, Derrida *et al*. Instead, Eisenstein draws on the language of universal democratic rights to 'demand' (not just argue) that they be transformed to include women of colour.

The Color of Gender appears over ten years after Zillah Eisenstein's influential text *The Radical Future of Liberal Feminism*, and she returns to the project of radicalizing the discourse of liberal rights, but from a different historical and political position. Reagan and Bush have been and gone, and the Clintons struggle on against the powerful legacy of the 1980s. The Soviet Union and its satellites have become 'post-communist', while feminism and radical Black politics are castigated as 'old-fashioned' at a time when civil rights and abortion law reforms have been all but destroyed in the USA. In this context, Eisenstein sets out to deconstruct the notion of universalism through a recognition that 'human rights' are always racialized, gendered and class-specific (and, I would add, sexualized). The 'universal rights' guaranteed by the 'founding fathers' of the nation were in effect those of the white male. Beginning instead from the imagined position of women of colour, Eisenstein rejects the pretence of universality embedded in the traditional discourses of human rights and individuality in order to rethink democracy, liberalism, socialism and feminism in the 1990s.

The bulk of the book examines five different political moments, four of which are located in the USA, in order to develop Eisenstein's reconstruction of democracy. The first such chapter considers the 'Eastern European male democracies' of the 'post-communist' years since 1989, examining these new patriarchal democracies and the implications for Eastern European feminism at a time of renewed racism and nationalism. Eisenstein argues that the recent struggles in Eastern Europe make it hard to imagine a democracy 'that is not patriarchal or torn apart by racial hatred'. Turning to the North American context, she envisions feminists as fighting for affirmative action policies that do not strive for sameness of treatment in aiming for racial and sexual equality. The next section starts by examining the dismantling of US civil rights legislation, the rise of an African American middle class and a Black male neo-conservatism in a detailed analysis of 'race', racism and civil rights law. Chapter 3 brings together the Civil Rights Act of 1990–91 with the Clarence Thomas–Anita Hill hearings, the Gulf War, the Los Angeles riots and 'Political Correctness' in an analysis of 'new racism' in the final part of the Bush administration up to the time of the Clinton victory. Chapter 4 focuses on legislation around abortion and reproductive rights during the Reagan–Bush era, especially with respect to 'the Webster decision' which upheld the right of a Missouri statute to limit the abortion rights of women. Eisenstein uses this example to strengthen her argument about the gradual privatization of the American state during this period. This section ends with an analysis of the contradictory politics around AIDS, where Eisenstein's focus on women of colour raises different questions in contrast to the usual concentration on white, middle-class, gay men. Examining the response of the Bush administration to this crisis, she also looks at the radical politics of ACTUP and the need for a 'revisioned radicalized democratic politics' that can address the racial, gendered, sexual and class-specific nature of the disease as well as its universal dimension. AIDS is not the sole province of gay or radical Black politics, any more than Black and gay (or Black and female) can be disentangled, but it *does* define and 'attack' specific communities. The detailed points of Eisenstein's text are sometimes available elsewhere, but the overall structure of her arguments about democracy, feminism, socialism and liberalism is important, and very much a product of and comment on its time. Eisenstein's perspective is located within the politics of Western democracies, especially the USA, although her words have relevance in other societies within similar cultural, political and economic traditions. Her concern is to write female bodies into democratic theory, and in the final chapter Eisenstein begins to make tentative connexions with the positions of women of colour outside the so-called 'First World'. She reviews the work of some white feminists and feminists of colour in their various understandings of feminism, difference, similarity, race, gender and class before ending on a note of guarded if determined optimism about the prospects for US politics after the first hundred days of the Clinton administration.

FEMINIST REVIEW NO 50, SUMMER 1995

The Color of Gender addresses important debates for feminists working in Western contexts. The relevance of the book is unlikely to be limited to the 1990s, not least because the questions addressed by Eisenstein will not easily be resolved. She sees these issues as challenges rather than unfortunate problems in an optimistic approach to politics which views conflict and contradiction as spurs to thought and action rather than as matters for embarrassment or retreat. One can only hope that her optimism is not too misplaced: according to Eisenstein we simply cannot afford it to be misplaced. I closed the book with a new (or renewed) appreciation of the need for an international feminist politics that dissolves the usual focus on First World contexts and recognizes the similarities and differences between women around the world. This is not the book that Eisenstein has written, but it is to her credit that *The Color of Gender*, despite its US focus, does not close off discussion but manages to leave the way open for further debate.

Christine Griffin

We're Rooted Here and They Can't Pull Us Up.
Essays in African Canadian Women's History
Coordinated by Peggy Bristow
University of Toronto Press: Canada, 1994
ISBN 0 820 6881 2

Rebellious slave woman and valiant fugitive. Devout Baptist church sister; abused, underpaid domestic; exploited wartime factory worker. Pioneering nurse and resolute teacher. 'Womanist' artist, academic and poet. African Canadian women emerge in this anthology in portraits which find parallels in other geographical areas of the African diaspora; they are punctuating their 400-year presence in Canada with testimony of their exclusion from and marginalization within Canadian life. These essays cover the history of African Canadian women from their arrival in the seventeenth century to the immediate post-war period. The relationship between the various organs of the state and Black women is a central theme and is discussed in the context of economic and social changes. The relations of African Canadian women to the Canadian economy are correctly both considered in the context of Black people in general and analysed in terms of gender, by the introduction of oral testimony, biographical sketches, analysis of census, government records and other official data.

Here is a panoramic documentation of women's experiences from the period of slavery which, as Sylvia Hamilton shows in the opening essay, 'was well entrenched before the arrival of the United Empire Loyalists in 1783'. Although the Black Loyalists believed they were coming to a land of liberty, they were frequently abused. Frustration led to mass migration to Sierra Leone, West Africa, just at the time when events in Jamaica, West Indies, led to the migration of the Maroons to Nova Scotia. Hamilton's interesting discussion adds a valuable dimension to the unfinished history of Black women in the diaspora and points to the need to weigh the correspondences between Black women's post-slavery cultural forms based on our growing knowledge of migration. Unchronicled journeys are also the subject of Adrienne Shand's essay on the Underground Movement.

Recognizing that the story of Harriet Tubman is already well known, Shand focuses on unsung heroines who escaped to Canada West before the American Civil War and explains the gender considerations of 'running away'. Motherhood, pregnancy and the more limited freedom of movement associated with domestic work forced many young slave women to stay put; however, there were exceptions such as Ann Marie Jackson who fled with her seven children, a pregnant woman who escaped in a box and others who 'cleverly donned suits of mourning' and eluded their owner!

Throughout *We're Rooted Here and They Can't Pull Us Up*, the reader is conscious of the difficulties these Black feminist scholars have faced in reconstructing this history. Their subjects have been ignored in white feminist histories such as Anita Clair Fellman's *Rethinking Canada: The Promise of Women's History* (1986) and even in popular Black histories the achievements of significant women are 'minimised' (p. 7). While such recent secondary sources are full of disappointments, the paucity of good primary sources continues to be the main drag. In Afua Cooper's portrait of the pioneer teacher Mary Bibb who began a school in 'a dark, ill-ventilated room' in her house in 1850, a handful of letters and newspaper reports are stitched together to show how Bibb coped with financial insecurity, government indifference and parental poverty in mid-nineteenth-century Sandwich. A broader sweep of this same period is taken by Peggy Bristow whose thorough account of women's experiences in Chatham and Buxton is grounded in a wider social/political history and explores the achievements of leaders such as journalist Mary Shadd Cary as well as community development, kinship and family structures, labour and cultural practice.

Finally, this century is discussed in the last two essays alone. Dionne Brand, using extensive oral testimony, gives a lively account of Black women's experiences in interwar Canada, showing how the racial/sexual division of labour militated against them and illustrating how women attempted to 'navigate the race barrier': 'Other times I would phone and they would say,

FEMINIST REVIEW NO 50, SUMMER 1995

"Well, are you dark?" and I would say, 'Well I'm not dark," and then they might say, "I'm sorry, the reason I'm asking is because we'd like our coloured help to be unquestionably coloured"' (p. 176).

Linda Carty revisits some of the material examined in earlier chapters, but adds in her discussion of the state, a section on immigration and the West Indian Domestic Scheme of 1955, which like British post-war measures set the stage for the present economic position of Black women.

Not surprisingly, this anthology brings us back to some of the images and ideas which we have come to expect from the Black feminist debate – the destructiveness of sexism and racism, the simultaneity of oppressions, the challenges of researching Black women in hostile environments, the need to make coalitions across the diaspora.

And so what?

All this is a necessary base for any group of Black feminist scholars to build upon and to which they can attach the specifics of their histories. In this way they generate 'knowledge' that is grounded in experience while happily boasting universal resonance.

Delia Jarrett-Macauley

Women & Change in the Caribbean: A Pan-Caribbean Perspective
Edited by Janet H. Momsen

Ian Randle Kingston: Indiana University Press Bloomington and Indianapolis; James Currey: London, 1993
ISBN 0 85255 403 6 £12.95 Pbk, ISBN 0 85255 404 4 £35.00 Hbk

The strength of this text resides in its refreshing insights into the myriad of Caribbean women's life experiences, many of which have previously been masked by the Eurocentric perceptions which blinker many scholars researching into this region; others have been blinkered by their 'gender blindness' regarding Black women. In historical and social sciences literature gender distinctions remain overshadowed by class and race consideration. In short gender, race and class limitations have prevented numerous scholars (as the text goes on to illustrate) from investigating the special dynamics reflected in Caribbean women's relationships.

The essays in this book are strongly supported by comprehensive field work which serves to bring together and challenge a number of misconceptions, in particular that of allocating Caribbean women's experiences to either the domain of the home or work spheres (public or private), without any understanding or appreciation of the importance of the interconnexions between these areas of women's lives. It is these 'gender specific interconnections' which, the contributors argue, provide crucial materials with which to understand how Caribbean women manage and negotiate their lives.

Women & Change in the Caribbean is divided into two distinct sections: 'Private & Public Spheres of Women's Lives' and 'Economic Roles of Caribbean Women'; both sections are further subdivided into two parts. I particularly enjoyed the first section of the book with its sociological emphasis, its concentration on women's active and creative interactions in implementing and maintaining structures which support their daily lives. The second section of the book examines gender division in agricultural production and the market economy.

Lydia Mihelic Pulsipher's piece on the 'Changing roles in the life cycles of women in traditional West Indian houseyards' offered a scintillating case study of a matriarchal base as an organizational structure, which operates to ensure continuity and support for family members. The interconnexions here indicate the nature of family support and the status ascribed to being a particular member of the 'yard'. Pulsipher contends that the organization and management of the houseyard is predominantly executed by women and is fundamental to the unwritten laws of inheritance, distribution of land and the maintenance of the family livelihood. Berleant-Schiller and Maurer's article on 'The merging domain and women's role in Barbuda and Dominica' and Bran-Shute's article on 'Neighbourhood networks and national politics among working-class Afro-Surinamese women', depict how women set up and utilize 'informal' networks to sustain and support their lives. 'Women's roles become integral to a range of social and economic processes that are not confined within the household' because the social importance of 'domestic' tasks places women in 'public' roles (Berleant-Schiller and Maurer, p. 65). These domains merge, both economically and ideologically (Berleant-Schiller and Maurer, p. 77) and the public–domestic dichotomy is not universally useful in explaining the various interconnexions which operate and are utilized by women in organizing their lives. What contributors in this section call for is to be engaged in less myopic observation and examine a whole different set of questions to be asked when studying Caribbean women's lives, roles and responsibilities.

Another successful unmasking achieved by this book is to make visible the contribution and participation of Caribbean women in agriculture. Christine Barrow, John S. Brierley, Indra S. Harry, Jean Stubbs and Janet

FEMINIST REVIEW NO 50, SUMMER 1995

H. Momsen illustrate and give due recognition to the special role women perform in agricultural production within the Caribbean region. In the case of Grenada, Brierley illustrates how sexism prevents acknowledgement being given to women's contribution to the production process. 'Farmers in Grenada have been the subject of several studies . . . while they refer to the fact that women head one in five small farm households, not one of these studies singled out the female component to determine what distinctive characteristics their farm possessed. . . . Yet the contributions of women farmers to social and economic development in Grenada are unquestionable and indispensable but, like those of women in other Third World nations, they have readily been taken for granted' (p. 194).

Momsen identified four factors she claims contributed to Caribbean women's high representation in the means of production. These are firstly the experience of performing much of the heaviest field labour under slavery; secondly access to land, which enabled many women to 'cultivate to feed their children'; thirdly 'out migration' from the Caribbean region, which caused many women to assume responsibility as head of household; and finally the availability of education which Momsen concludes, 'is seen by women as their main source of security' (p. 232). These features, Momsen maintains, have contributed to the Caribbean region as having 'one of the highest levels of female economic activity rates and education in the so-called developing world' (p. 3).

These essays add their voices to the growing number of Black feminist researchers emanating from the region (see p. 3), and show the need, not only to make visible but also to acknowledge the lessons which can be learnt from Caribbean women's experiences in the region.

Another orthodoxy challenged here is the inclusion of 'communities of women' not often brought together in studies. Some of these are: Afro-Surinamese working-class women; the migratory experiences of women from the area; Sephardic women of Curacao; and women's role in political organizations. Articles also spanned the Franco, Hispanic, and Anglophone Caribbean communities and this should be credited as another attempt to challenge regional chauvinism, gender invisibility and marginalization of Caribbean women.

It would have been useful to have the text illustrated with maps of the region. Almost every chapter needed its own specific detailed map to help the reader pinpoint the physical areas under discussion. Given the number of geographers and anthropologists contributing to the work, this diversity should have been celebrated with visual representation of the region.

Women & Change in the Caribbean presents a number of challenges to scholars, and the contributors make a case for studying the experiences of Caribbean women that challenges Eurocentric and sexist perceptions and points the way forward. It also boldly presents a Black perspective in which the women need to be seen, studied and reflected upon with insight and understanding.

The incisive and stimulating studies revealed by the contributors showed women's capacity to construct, negotiate and develop their lives in creative, diverse and extraordinary ways.

I am pleased to say the author succeeded in presenting some very insightful, stimulating new material, strongly supported by active field research.

Claudette Williams

Compañeras: Voices from the Latin American Women's Movement
Edited by Gaby Küppers
Latin American Bureau: London, 1994
ISBN 0 906156 86 6, £8.99/$15.00 Pbk

Compañeras is the latest addition to the important new series of books on Latin America's women's movements from the Latin American Bureau. The series is especially welcome in Britain where the interest in Latin American politics and societies is growing. So, first let me record my thanks to the Latin American Bureau and encourage *Feminist Review* readers to make contact with and support the work of the Bureau. Raising the profile of Latin America is no easy task and overcoming the exoticization of the diverse cultures and peoples that are encompassed by this imaginary, 'Latin America', an even harder one. But, as the writings of Latin American intellectuals and activists do become available to English-speaking readers, they are offered a vision of the world far more optimistic than their own and one in which, despite the traumatic histories of Latin American states, the discourses within which politics is constructed are novel and affirmative. This is clearly evidenced in *Compañeras*.

The book, introduced by Gaby Küppers, is an inspiring set of interviews with women throughout Latin America, from the Andean cultures of Bolivia and Peru to the Caribbean of Haiti and the complexities of Brazil, Colombia and Cuba. The collection itself speaks for the diversity of the region and the growing sense of a Latin–Caribbean identity which is fuelled by shared politics and literature debated at the numerous women's events across the region. The interviews are organized around a series of themes that have resonances both globally and locally. The first of these is the question of autonomy for feminist and women's activism followed by the debate around the role of women in the social movements. The two come together in the third theme, 'Reclaiming Politics', the attempt to generate and support a feminist agenda within the political parties. Fourth is the vital articulation between human rights and women's rights. The final sections concern feminist publications and the future – 'Where Next?' The themes are intended as a starting point because, as the editor suggests, the collection is an open-ended one like the politics it seeks to convey.

Throughout the interviews there is no sense that women's movements in Latin America can speak with one voice or through a homogenized account of 'woman'. While some may be womanist the first recognition is the diversity of women and how this diversity is lived and theorized within the articulations of racism, sexism, class relations and the state. The issue of sexuality and heterosexism still remains contained within discourses on reproductive rights and is constructed within a terrain of meaning and practice hegemonized by the Church and the State. It is also clear that the women interviewed do not seek to romanticize feminist and women's politics or make extravagant claims for feminist agendas. As Maria Dirlene T. Marques, an activist in the Workers' Party of Brazil notes, 'The women's movement in Brazil is in an extremely bad state. There are feminists but no functioning feminist movement.' Maria, at the time of the interview, was the only woman member of the regional council of the party and noted that the ratio of men to women in positions of power was 20 to 1. But the party did vote for a form of positive discrimination for women in 1991 suggesting that all committees should have 30 per cent women members. The workers' movements in Latin America, within both political parties and trade unions, have provided a difficult but important space of contestation for women activists as the interviews attest; one in which issues and policies that respond to feminist questions and demands can be fought over.

But the issue of 'feminism' is still a complex one and as the interviews show often goes unnamed as part of the difficulties of using a language which was, in part, imported and did not seem to address the issues faced by women or the structures which came to bear upon their lives. As Maritza Villavicencio, a Peruvian woman, writes: 'For the women's movement today, terrorism and state repression are the second most important issue after the economic crisis' (p. 69). This is part of the story for so many of the women interviewed in the book. The women from Guatemala and El Salvador have, since the eighties, organized women's projects including a refuge and sought to intervene at the local level in areas of health, income generation and safety against state terror. But, as is clear from the Brazilian activist Maria Amelia Teles, local struggles are vitally important but national politics intervenes especially in relation to reproductive rights. She records that: 'Officially, 25 million women have been sterilised, many of them between 15 and 19 years old. That represents a kind of preventative genocide' (p. 75) and Maria Amelia concludes, 'There was never any sexual freedom for women, never any right to desire, never any right to decide freely whether they wanted to have children or not. So the right to choose is our motto and a great dream of ours' (p. 77).

Given the hostile terrain in which women seek to forge their politics, dreams are a crucial part of the ways in which women in Latin America and the Caribbean come together to forge collective subjects as a basis for action, whether in relation to workers' rights, political programmes or the interventions in the forms of communication like the Peruvian journal *Mujer y Sociedad* first published in 1980 and now appearing monthly as a supplement in the daily newspaper *La República. Cotidiano Mujer* from Uruguay began in 1985 and also considered being part of a national daily but found this untenable and now publishes independently. There are feminist magazines and more specialist poetry and art magazines throughout Latin America as well as mujer/fempress, a Latin American women's news agency. These journals and the shared newsline are a vital part of the cross-border communications which sustain women's organizing and cultural production within a great variety of political contexts from the universities and local radio to the grassroots movements.

The costs of an active engagement are poignantly expressed in the interview with Eulalia Yagari Gonzalez, an indigenous woman from Colombia, when she says, 'the right to love and politics', a view detailed in the interview where she expresses the regret that her political engagement means distance from her daughters cared for by relatives and a 'difficult relationship' with a politically active partner. 'We love each other but our political struggle in this quagmire of violence and war makes it impossible for couples to live in peace with one another . . . Commitment to the cause takes away the ability and the time for love' (p. 141). This book is a testament to these sacrifices and to the ways in which women throughout Latin America and the Caribbean keep alive the dream of love and politics. I am humble in the face of the determination and strength in these chapters and inspired by the commitment, energy and the place of love and the ways of the heart in the women's lives. In part this is set within a discourse of rights but as Esther Andradi, an Argentinian woman, emphasizes, 'the right to be at peace with oneself and the right to pleasure. By no means is pleasure at the end of our list of demands: it is implicit in all our actions, in

FEMINIST REVIEW NO 50, SUMMER 1995

our groups and our togetherness. It is the pleasure which grows from a sense that we are no longer alone. Never again' (p. 6).

This book is a very important book, giving texture and voice to the debates on the role of women in the social movements in Latin America and the Caribbean and to the theorization and practice of postmodern politics.

Contact the Latin American Bureau at 1 Amwell Street, London EC1R 1UL.

Sallie Westwood

Letter

FEMINIST REVIEW NO 50, SUMMER 1995

Dear *Feminist Review*

I am writing to express my concern at the unpleasant tone of Janet Rachel's review of *Gender & Technology in the Making* by Cynthia Cockburn and Susan Ormrod. I believe that as a matter of developing a tolerant exchange between feminist scholars it should be unacceptable to conclude a review with the sentence: 'It is to these skills that we must attend if we are to be anything other than technically incompetent badge wearing feminists'.

It happens that as a feminist sociologist of science, and to some extent technology, I think the Cockburn and Ormrod book is stunningly good, and that I suspect an enormous number of feminists and others will get great intellectual pleasure from reading it. But the difference in our evaluation of the text is a matter of judgement. For example, in my view it is sheer dualistic rot to suggest, as Rachel does, that it is impossible 'to claim both Harding and Haraway as equally relevant to the study'. Any careful reading of the exchanges between these two would see the mutually shaping conversation developing between them. But the proof of the pudding is in the eating, not in a sour review. Go read.

Yours sincerely,

Hilary Rose,
Institute of Education,
18 Woburn Square, London WC1H 0NS

Noticeboard

FEMINIST REVIEW NO 51, AUTUMN 1995, pp. 154–154

Call for Papers

The Journal of International Communication

Special Issue: *International Feminism(s)* (June 1996) Guest edited by Prof. Annabelle Sreberny-Mohammadi.

This issue is devoted to an exploration of international feminism(s) as theoretical constructs, practical politics, cultural practices. Articles that combine such kinds of analysis, and also provide comparative or 'global' perspectives, are particularly welcome. Contributions are invited from across and among (and outside) academic disciplines.

Proposals should be sent to and Notes for Contributors requested from the Guest Editor at the following address: Prof. Annabelle Sreberny-Mohammadi, Director, Centre for Mass Communication Research, University of Leicester, 104 Regent Road, Leicester LE1 7LT, England. Tel: 44-116-2523861/3; Fax: 44-116-2523874; E-mail: as19@leicester.ac.uk. Deadline: 30 September 1995.

Announcements

Garnet publishing launches: The Arab Women Writers Series

An important series presenting the best of contemporary fiction from the Middle East (Series Editor, Fadia Faqir).

This new series aims to bring Western readers the best of contemporary fiction from a range of countries across the Middle East, and the first four novels have been chosen to reflect the diversity of experiences in the Middle East.

Following the Gulf War, and after reflecting on the profound lack of cross-cultural understanding which she felt had contributed to this, series editor Dr Fadia Faqir decided to present a broader view which would help Europeans to a better, and less suspicious, understanding of Arabs and the Middle East.

Titles include: *The Stone of Laughter* by Hoda Barakat (Lebanon); *The Golden Chariot* by Salwa Bakr (Egypt); *The Homeland* by Hamida Na'na (Syria); and *The Eye of the Mirror* by Liana Badr (Palestine). All titles published 27 April 1995, 240 pages, £8.95.

If you need further information on any title in this series, please contact: Alex Walker, Publicist, 4 Oakey Close, Alvescot, Oxfordshire OX18 2PX. Fax and Tel: (01993) 846255.

FEMINIST REVIEW NO 51, AUTUMN 1995, pp. 156–164

1 Women and Revolution in South Yemen, **Molyneux**. Feminist Art Practice, **Davis & Goodal**. Equal Pay and Sex Discrimination, **Snell**. Female Sexuality in Fascist Ideology, **Macciocchi**. Charlotte Brontë's *Shirley*, **Taylor**. Christine Delphy, **Barrett & McIntosh**. OUT OF PRINT.

2 Summer Reading, **O'Rourke**. Disaggregation, **Campaign for Legal and Financial Independence** and **Rights of Women**. The Hayward Annual 1978, **Pollock**. Women and the Cuban Revolution, **Murray**. Matriarchy Study Group Papers, **Lee**. Nurseries in the Second World War, **Riley**.

3 English as a Second Language, **Naish**. Women as a Reserve Army of Labour, **Bruegel**. Chantal Akerman's films, **Martin**. Femininity in the 1950s, **Birmingham Feminist History Group**. On Patriarchy, **Beechey**. Board School Reading Books, **Davin**.

4 Protective Legislation, **Coyle**. Legislation in Israel, **Yuval-Davis**. On 'Beyond the Fragments', **Wilson**. Queen Elizabeth I, **Heisch**. Abortion Politics: a dossier. Materialist Feminism, **Delphy**.

5 Feminist Sexual Politics, **Campbell**. Iranian Women, **Tabari**. Women and Power, **Stacey & Price**. Women's Novels, **Coward**. Abortion, **Himmelweit**. Gender and Education, **Nava**. Sybilla Aleramo, **Caesar**. On 'Beyond the Fragments', **Margolis**.

6 'The Tidy House', **Steedman**. Writings on Housework, **Kaluzynska**. The Family Wage, **Land**. Sex and Skill, **Phillips & Taylor**. Fresh Horizons, **Lovell**. Cartoons, **Hay**.

7 Protective Legislation, **Humphries**. Feminists Must Face the Future, **Coultas**. Abortion in Italy, **Caldwell**. Women's Trade Union Conferences, **Breiten-bach**. Women's Employment in the Third World, **Elson & Pearson**

8 Socialist Societies Old and New, **Molyneux**. Feminism and the Italian Trade Unions, **Froggett & Torchi**. Feminist Approach to Housing in Britain, **Austerberry & Watson**. Psychoanalysis, **Wilson**. Women in the Soviet Union, **Buckley**. The Struggle within the Struggle, **Kimble**.

9 Position of Women in Family Law, **Brophy & Smart**. Slags or Drags, **Cowie & Lees**. The Ripper and Male Sexuality, **Hollway**. The Material of Male Power, **Cockburn**. Freud's *Dora*, **Moi**. Women in an Iranian Village, **Afshar**. New Office Technology and Women, **Morgall**.

10 Towards a Wages Strategy for Women, **Weir & McIntosh**. Irish Suffrage Movement, **Ward**. A Girls' Project and Some Responses to Lesbianism, **Nava**. The Case for Women's Studies, **Evans**. Equal Pay and Sex Discrimination, **Gregory**. Psychoanalysis and Personal Politics, **Sayers**.

11 **Sexuality issue**
Sexual Violence and Sexuality, **Coward**. Interview with Andrea Dworkin, **Wilson**. The Dyke, the Feminist and the Devil, **Clark**. Talking Sex, **English, Hollibaugh & Rubin**. Jealousy and Sexual Difference, **Moi**. Ideological Politics 1969–72, **O'Sullivan**. Womanslaughter in the Criminal Law, **Radford**. OUT OF PRINT.

12 ANC Women's Struggles, **Kimble & Unterhalter**. Women's Strike in Holland 1981, **de Bruijn & Henkes**. Politics of Feminist Research, **McRobbie**. Khomeini's Teachings on Women, **Afshar**. Women in the Labour Party 1906–1920, **Rowan**. Documents from the Indian Women's Movement, **Gothoskar & Patel**.

13 Feminist Perspectives on Sport, **Graydon**. Patriarchal Criticism and Henry James, **Kappeler**. The Barnard Conference on Sexuality, **Wilson**. Danger and Pleasure in Nineteenth Century Feminist Sexual Thought, **Gordon & Du Bois**. Anti-Porn: Soft Issue, Hard World, **Rich**. Feminist Identity and Poetic Tradition, **Montefiore**.

14 Femininity and its Discontents, **Rose**. Inside and Outside Marriage, **Gittins**. The Pro-family Left in the United States, **Epstein & Ellis**. Women's Language and Literature, **McKluskie**. The Inevitability of Theory, **Fildes**. The 150 Hours in Italy, **Caldwell**. Teaching Film, **Clayton**.

15 Women's Employment, **Beechey**. Women and Trade Unions, **Charles**. Lesbianism and Women's Studies, **Adamson**. Teaching Women's Studies at Secondary School, **Kirton**. Gender, Ethnic and Class Divisions, **Anthias & Yuval-Davis**. Women Studying or Studying Women, **Kelly & Pearson**. Girls, Jobs and Glamour, **Sherratt**. Contradictions in Teaching Women's Studies, **Phillips & Hurstfield**.

16 Romance Fiction, Female Sexuality and Class, **Light**. The White Brothel, **Kappeler**. Sadomasochism and Feminism, **France**. Trade Unions and Socialist Feminism, **Cockburn**. Women's Movement and the Labour Party, **Interview with Labour Party Feminists**. Feminism and 'The Family', **Caldwell**.

17 Many voices, one chant: black feminist perspectives

Challenging Imperial Feminism, **Amos & Parmar**. Black Women, the Economic Crisis and the British State, **Mama**. Asian Women in the Making of History, **Trivedi**. Black Lesbian Discussions, **Carmen, Gail, Shaila & Pratibha**. Poetry. Black Women Organizing Autonomously: a collection.

18 Cultural politics

Writing with Women. A Metaphorical Journey, **Lomax**. Karen Alexander: Video Worker, **Nava**. Poetry by **Riley, Whiteson** and **Davies**. Women's Films, **Montgomery**. 'Correct Distance' a photo-text, **Tabrizian**. Julia Kristeva on Femininity, **Jones**. Feminism and the Theatre, **Wandor**. Alexis Hunter, **Osborne**. Format Photographers, Dear Linda, **Kuhn**.

19

The Female Nude in the work of Suzanne Valadon, **Betterton**. Refuges for Battered Women, **Pahl**. Thin is the Feminist Issue, **Diamond**. New Portraits for Old, **Martin & Spence**.

20

Prisonhouses, **Steedman**. Ethnocentrism and Socialist Feminism, **Barrett & McIntosh**. What Do Women Want? **Rowbotham**. Women's Equality and the European Community, **Hoskyns**. Feminism and the Popular Novel of the 1890s, **Clarke**.

21

Going Private: The Implications of Privatization for Women's Work, **Coyle**. A Girl Needs to Get Street-wise: Magazines for the 1980s, **Winship**. Family Reform in Socialist States: The Hidden Agenda, **Molyneux**. Sexual Segregation in the Pottery Industry, **Sarsby**.

22

Interior Portraits: Women, Physiology and the Male Artist, **Pointon**. The Control of Women's Labour: The Case of Homeworking, **Allen & Wolkowitz**. Homeworking: Time for Change, **Cockpit Gallery & Londonwide Homeworking Group**. Feminism and Ideology: The Terms of Women's Stereotypes, **Seiter**. Feedback: Feminism and Racism, **Ramazanoglu, Kazi, Lees, Safia Mirza**.

23 Socialist-feminism: out of the blue

Feminism and Class Politics: A Round-Table Discussion, **Barrett, Campbell, Philips, Weir & Wilson**. Upsetting an Applecart: Difference, Desire and Lesbian Sadomasochism, **Ardill & O'Sullivan**. Armagh and Feminist Strategy, **Loughran**. Transforming Socialist-Feminism: The Challenge of Racism, **Bhavnani & Coulson**. Socialist-Feminists and Greenham, **Finch & Hackney Greenham Groups**. Socialist-Feminism and the Labour Party: Some Experiences from Leeds, **Perrigo**. Some Political Implications of Women's Involvement in the Miners' Strike 1984–85, **Rowbotham & McCrindle**. Sisterhood: Political Solidarity Between Women, **Hooks**. European Forum of Socialist-Feminists, **Lees & McIntosh**. Report from Nairobi, **Hendessi**.

24 Women Workers in New Industries in Britain, **Glucksmann.** The Relationship of Women to Pornography, **Bower.** The Sex Discrimination Act 1975, **Atkins.** The Star Persona of Katharine Hepburn, **Thumim.**

25 Difference: A Special Third World Women Issue, **Minh-ha.** Melanie Klein, Psychoanalysis and Feminism, **Sayers.** Rethinking Feminist Attitudes Towards Mothering, **Gieve.** EEOC v. Sears, Roebuck and Company: A Personal Account, **Kessler-Harris.** Poems, **Wood.** Academic Feminism and the Process of De-radicalization, **Currie & Kazi.** A Lover's Distance: A Photoessay, **Boffin.**

26 Resisting Amnesia: Feminism, Painting and Post-Modernism, **Lee.** The Concept of Difference, **Barrett.** The Weary Sons of Freud, **Clément.** Short Story, **Cole.** Taking the Lid Off: Socialist Feminism in Oxford, **Collette.** For and Against the European Left: Socialist Feminists Get Organized, **Benn.** Women and the State: A Conference of Feminist Activists, **Weir.**

27 Women, feminism and the third term
Women and Income Maintenance, **Lister.** Women in the Public Sector, **Phillips.** Can Feminism Survive a Third Term?, **Loach.** Sex in Schools, **Wolpe.** Carers and the Careless, **Doyal.** Interview with Diane Abbott, **Segal.** The Problem With No Name: Re-reading Friedan, **Bowlby.** Second Thoughts on the Second Wave, **Rosenfelt & Stacey.** Nazi Feminists?, **Gordon.**

28 Family secrets: child sexual abuse
Introduction to an Issue: Family Secrets as Public Drama, **McIntosh.** Challenging the Orthodoxy: Towards a Feminist Theory and Practice, **MacLeod & Saraga.** The Politics of Child Sexual Abuse: Notes from American History, **Gordon.** What's in a Name?: Defining Child Sexual Abuse, **Kelly.** A Case, **Anon.** Defending Innocence: Ideologies of Childhood, **Kitzinger.** Feminism and the Seductiveness of the 'Real Event', **Scott.** Cleveland and the Press: Outrage and Anxiety in the Reporting of Child Sexual Abuse, **Nava.** Child Sexual Abuse and the Law, **Woodcraft.** Poem, **Betcher.** Brixton Black Women's Centre: Organizing on Child Sexual Abuse, **Bogle.** Bridging the Gap: Glasgow Women's Support Project, **Bell & MacLeod.** Claiming Our Status as Experts: Community Organizing, **Norwich Consultants on Sexual Violence.** Islington Social Services: Developing a Policy on Child Sexual Abuse, **Boushel & Noakes.** Developing a Feminist School Policy on Child Sexual Abuse, **O'Hara.** 'Putting Ideas into their Heads': Advising the Young, **Mills.** Child Sexual Abuse Crisis Lines: Advice for Our British Readers.

29 Abortion: the international agenda
Whatever Happened to 'A Woman's Right to Choose'?, **Berer.** More than 'A Woman's Right to Choose'?, **Himmelweit.** Abortion in the Republic of Ireland, **Barry.** Across the Water, **Irish Women's Abortion Support Group.** Spanish Women and the Alton Bill, **Spanish Women's Abortion Support Group.** The Politics of Abortion in Australia: Freedom, Church and State, **Coleman.** Abortion in Hungary, **Szalai.** Women and Population Control in China: Issues of Sexuality, Power and Control, **Hillier.** The Politics of Abortion in Nicaragua: Revolutionary Pragmatism –

Field. Mapping: Lesbians, AIDS and Sexuality: An Interview with Cindy Patton, O'Sullivan. Significant Others: Lesbians and Psychoanalytic Theory, Hamer. The Pleasure Threshold: Looking at Lesbian Pornography on Film, Smyth. Cartoon, Charlesworth. Voyages of the Valkyries: Recent Lesbian Pornographic Writing, Dunn.

35 Campaign Against Pornography, Norden. The Mothers' Manifesto and Disputes over 'Mutterlichkeit', Chamberlayne. Multiple Mediations: Feminist Scholarship in the Age of Multi-National Reception, Mani. Cagney and Lacey Revisited, Alcock & Robson. Cutting a Dash: The Dress of Radclyffe Hall and Una Troubridge, Rolley. Deviant Dress, Wilson. The House that Jill Built: Lesbian Feminist Organizing in Toronto, 1976–1980, Ross. Women in Professional Engineering: the Interaction of Gendered Structures and Values, Carter & Kirkup. Identity Politics and the Hierarchy of Oppression, Briskin. Poetry: Bufkin, Zumwalt.

36 'The Trouble Is It's Ahistorical': The Problem of the Unconscious in Modern Feminist Theory, Minsky. Feminism and Pornography, Ellis, O'Dair and Tallmer. Who Watches the Watchwomen? Feminists Against Censorship, Rodgerson & Semple. Pornography and Violence: What the 'Experts' Really Say, Segal. The Woman In My Life: Photography of Women, Nava. Splintered Sisterhood: Anti-racism in a Young Women's Project, Connolly. Woman, Native, Other, Parmar interviews Trinh T. Minh-ha. Out But Not Down: Lesbians' Experience of Housing, Edgerton. Poems: Evans Davies, Toth, Weinbaum. Oxford Twenty Years On: Where Are We Now?, Gamman & O'Neill. The Embodiment of Ugliness and the Logic of Love: The Danish Redstockings Movement, Walter.

37 Theme issue: Women, religion and dissent
Black Women, Sexism and Racism: Black or Antiracist Feminism?, Tang Nain. Nursing Histories: Reviving Life in Abandoned Selves, McMahon. The Quest for National Identity: Women, Islam and the State of Bangladesh, Kabeer. Born Again Moon: Fundamentalism in Christianity and the Feminist Spirituality Movement, McCrickard. Washing our Linen: One Year of Women Against Fundamentalism, Connolly. Siddiqui on *Letter to Christendom*, Bard on *Generations of Memories*, Patel on *Women Living Under Muslim Laws Dossiers 1–6*, Poem, Kay. More Cagney and Lacey, Gamman.

38 The Modernist Style of Susan Sontag, McRobbie. Tantalizing Glimpses of Stolen Glances: Lesbians Take Photographs, Fraser and Boffin. Reflections on the Women's Movement in Trinidad, Mohammed. Fashion, Representation and Femininity, Evans & Thornton. The European Women's Lobby, Hoskyns. Hendessi on *Law of Desire: Temporary Marriage in Iran*, Kaveney on *Mercy*.

39 Shifting territories: feminism & Europe
Between Hope and Helplessness: Women in the GDR, Dölling. Where Have All the Women Gone? Women and the Women's Movement in East Central Europe, Einborn. The End of Socialism in Europe – A New Challenge For Socialist Feminism?, Haug. The Second 'No': Women in Hungary, Kiss. The Citizenship

and Renaming: New Cartographies of Identity, Gender and Landscape in Ireland, **Nash**. Rap Poem: Easter 1991, **Medbh**. Family Feuds: Gender, Nationalism and the Family, **McClintock**. Women as Activists; Women as Symbols: A Study of the Indian Nationalist Movement, **Thapar**. Gender, Nationalisms and National Identities: Bellagio Symposium Report, **Hall**. Culture or Citizenship? Notes from the Gender and Colonialism Conference, Galway, Ireland, May 1992, **Connolly**. Reviews.

45 Thinking through ethnicities
Audre Lorde: Reflections. Re-framing Europe: Engendered Racisms, Ethnicities and Nationalisms in Contemporary Western Europe, **Brah**. Towards a Multicultural Europe? 'Race' Nation and Identity in 1992 and Beyond, **Bhavnani**. Another View: Photo Essay, **Pollard**. Growing Up White: Feminism, Racism and the Social Geography of Childhood, **Frankenberg**. Poem, **Kay**. Looking Beyond the Violent Break-up of Yugoslavia, **Coulson**. Personal Reactions of a Bosnian Woman to the War in Bosnia, **Harper**. Serbian Nationalism: Nationalism of My Own People, **Korac**. Belgrade Feminists 1992: Separation, Guilt and Identity Crisis, **Mladjenovic** and **Litricin**. Report on a Council of Europe Minority Youth Committee Seminar on Sexism and Racism in Western Europe, **Walker**. Reviews.

46 Sexualities: challenge and change
Chips, Coke and Rock-'n-Roll: Children's Mediation of an Invitation to a First Dance Party, **Rossiter**. Power and Desire: The Embodiment of Female Sexuality, **Holland, Ramazanoglu, Sharpe, Thomson**. Two Poems, **Janzen**. A Girton Girl on the Throne: Queen Christina and Versions of Lesbianism 1906–1933. Changing Interpretations of the Sexuality of Queen Christina of Sweden, **Waters**. The Pervert's Progress: An Analysis of 'The Story of O' and The Beauty Trilogy, **Ziv**. Dis-Graceful Images: Della Grace and Lesbian Sadomasochism, **Lewis**. Reviews.

47
Virgin Territories and Motherlands: Colonial and Nationalist Representations of Africa, **Innes**. The Impact of the Islamic Movement in Egypt, **Shukrallah**. Mothering on the Lam: Politics, Gender Fantasies and Maternal Thinking in Women Associated with Armed, Clandestine Organizations in the US, **Zwerman**. Treading the Traces of Discarded History: Photo-Essay, **Marchant**. The Feminist Production of Knowledge: Is Deconstruction a Practice for Women?, **Nash**. 'Divided We Stand': Sex, Gender and Sexual Difference, **Moore**. Reviews.

48 Sex and the state
Editorial. Not Just (Any) *Body* Can be a Citizen: The Politics of Law, Sexuality and Postcoloniality in Trinidad and Tobago and the Bahamas, **Alexander**. State, Family and Personal Responsibility: The Changing Balance for Lone Mothers in the United Kingdom, **Millar**. Moral Rhetoric and Public Health Pragmatism: The Recent Politics of Sex Education, **Thomson**. Through the Parliamentary Looking Glass: 'Real' and 'Pretend' Families in Contemporary British Politics, **Reinhold**. In Search of Gender Justice: Sexual Assault and the Criminal Justice System, **Gregory and Lees**. God's Bullies: Attacks on Abortion, **Hadley**. Sex Work, HIV and the State: an Interview with Nel Druce, **Overs**. Reviews.

FEMINIST REVIEW NO 51, AUTUMN 1995

49 Feminist politics – Colonial/postcolonial worlds

Women on the March: Right-Wing Mobilization in Contemporary India, **Mazumdar**. Colonial Encounters in Late-Victorian England: Pandita Ramabai at Cheltenham and Wantage, **Burton**. Subversive Intent: A Social Theory of Gender, **Maharaj**. My Discourse/My Self: Therapy as Possibility (for women who eat compulsively), **Hopwood**. Poems, **Donohue**. Review Essays. Reviews.

50 The Irish issue: the British question

Editorial. Deconstructing Whiteness: Irish Women in Britain, **Hickman and Walter**. Poem, **Smyth**. States of Change: Reflections of Ireland in Several Uncertain Parts, **Smyth**. Silences: Irish Women and Abortion, **Fletcher**. Poem, **Higgins**. Irish Women Poets and the Iconic Feminine, **Mills**. Irish/Woman/Artwork: Selective Readings, **Robinson**. Self-Determination: The Republican Feminist Agenda, **Hackett**. Ourselves Alone? Clár na mBan Conference Report, **Connolly**. Conflicting Interests: The British and Irish Suffrage Movements, **Ward**. Women Disarmed: The Militarization of Politics in Ireland 1913–23, **Benton**. 'The Crying Game', **Edge**.

Feminist Review was founded in 1979. Since that time it has established itself as one of the UK's leading feminist journals.

• Why not subscribe?
Make sure of your copy

All subscriptions run in calendar years. The issues for 1995 are Nos. 49, 50 and 51. You will save over £5 pa on the single copy price.

• Subscription rates, 1995 (3 issues)

Individual Subscriptions

UK/EEC	£24
Overseas	£30
North America	$42

A number of reduced cost (£15.50 per year: UK only) subscriptions are available for readers experiencing financial hardship, e.g. unemployed, student, low-paid. If you'd like to be considered for a reduced subscription, please write to the Collective, c/o the Feminist Review office, 52 Featherstone Street, London EC1Y 8RT.

Institutional Subscriptions		Single Issues	
UK	£68	UK	£8.99
Overseas	£74	North America	$12.95
North America	$110		

☐ Please send me one year's subscription to **Feminist Review**
☐ Please send me _____ copies of back issue no. _____

METHOD OF PAYMENT
☐ I enclose a cheque/international money order to the value of _____
  made payable to Routledge Journals
☐ Please charge my Access/Visa/American Express/Diners Club account

Account no. ☐☐☐☐☐☐☐☐☐☐☐☐☐☐☐☐☐☐

Expiry date _____ Signature _____

If the address below is different from the registered address of your credit card, please give your registered address separately.
PLEASE USE BLOCK CAPITALS
Name _____
Address_____
_____
_____
_____ Postcode _____
☐ Please send me a Routledge Journals Catalogue
☐ Please send me a Routledge Gender and Women's Studies Catalogue

Please return this form with payment to:
Routledge Subscriptions Department, Cheriton House, North Way, Andover, Hants SP10 5BE

Routledge titles are available from good bookshops or can be ordered direct from our Customer Hotline on **01264 342923.**

For more information please contact Ed Ripley at Routledge, 11 New Fetter Lane, London, EC4P 4EE. Tel: **0171 842 2158** or E-mail **info@routledge.com**

The Routledge catalogue is available on the Internet by accessing **http://www.routledge.com/routledge.html**

ROUTLEDGE
Drama & Literature

Contemporary Plays by Women of Color
AN ANTHOLOGY

Edited by **Kathy A. Perkins** and **Roberta Uno**

A collection of previously unpublished new and recent works by US women playwrights of colour. Featuring biographical notes on each writer and the production history of each play, this is a unique resource for practitioners and students.

January 1996: illus.18 b+w photos
Hb: 0-415-11377-6: **£45.00** Pb: 0-415-11378-4:**£14.99**

Fear of the Dark
'RACE', GENDER AND SEXUALITY IN THE CINEMA

Lola Young

The first scholarly study of race, gender and sexuality in European cinema, Fear of the Dark provides a lively, authoritative, and sometimes controversial analysis, questioning the extent to which black film makers have challenged stereotypes.

Gender, Racism, Ethnicity Series
November 1995: 224pp
Hb: 0-415-09709-6: **£37.50** Pb: 0-415-09710-X:**£12.99**

Renaissance Woman
A SOURCEBOOK CONSTRUCTIONS OF FEMININITY IN ENGLAND

Edited by **Kate Aughterson**

An invaluable collection of critically-informed accounts of women and feminity in early modern England. The volume brings together sources ranging from political pamphlets and medical documents to sermons and the bible, providing a historical context to issues of gender in the Renaissance.

October 1995: 248pp
Hb: 0-415-12045-4: **£45.00** Pb: 0-415-12046-2:**£14.99**

Renaissance Drama by Women
TEXTS AND DOCUMENTS

Edited by **Susan Cerasano** and **Marion Wynne-Davies**

Renaissance Drama by Women demonstrates the wide range of theatrical activity in which women were involved during the Renaissance period. It includes full-length plays, a translated fragment by Queen Elizabeth I, a masque and a substantial number of historical documents.

November 1995: 224pp: illus.6 b+w photos
Hb: 0-415-09806-8: **£40.00** Pb: 0-415-09807-6:**£12.99**

Women's Poetry of the 1930s
A CRITICAL ANTHOLOGY

Edited by **Jane Dowson**

In *Women's Poetry of the 1930s'*, Jane Dowson recovers women's place in the literary history of the interwar years and demands a reassessment of 1930s poetry. This comprehensive and beautifully edited collection will be an invaluable resource and a treasured volume for students, scholars and poetry enthuiasts alike.

November 1995:
Hb: 0-415-13095-6: **£35.00** Pb: 0-415-13096-4: **£8.99**

ROUTLEDGE
Anthropology

Routledge titles are available from good bookshops or can be ordered direct from our Customer Hotline on **01264 342923.**

For more information please contact Valerie Rose at Routledge, 11 New Fetter Lane, London, EC4P 4EE. Tel: **0171 842 2184** or E-mail **info@routledge.com**

The Routledge catalogue is available on the Internet by accessing **http://www.routledge.com/routledge.html**

Beyond the Masks
RACE, GENDER AND SUBJECTIVITY
Amina Mama

Incisive and readable account of black subjectivity. Amina Mama examines the history of imperial psychology and the ways in which the discipline has propagated racism. Offering an important theoretical perspective Beyond the Masks will appeal to all those studying ethnicity, gender and questions of identity.

Critical Psychology Series
August 1995:
Hb: 0-415-03543-0: **£40.00**

Gender Rituals
FEMALE INITIATION IN MELANESIA
Edited by **Nancy C Lutkehaus** and **Paul B Roscoe**

A discussion of ethnographies of female initiation rites in Melanesia which requires anthropologists to rethink their analysis of initiations and their perceptions of gender.

October 1995: illus.12 illustrations
Hb: 0-415-91106-0: **£37.50** Pb: 0-415-91107-9: **£13.99**

Gendering Orientalism
RACE, FEMININITY AND REPRESENTATION
Reina Lewis

By revealing the extent of women's involvement in the field of visual Orientalism and highlighting the presence of Orientalist themes in the work of Henriette Browne, George Eliot and Charlotte Brönte, the author uncovers women's roles in imperial culture and discourse.

Gender, Racism, Ethnicity Series
November 1995: illus.40 photos
Hb: 0-415-12489-1: **£40.00**: Pb: 0-415-12490-5: **£13.99**

White Women, Race Matters
THE SOCIAL CONSTRUCTION OF WHITENESS
Ruth Frankenberg

With extracts from in-depth life history interviews, this unique book examines the experiences practices and assumptions of white women in a racially hierarchical society.

'Disturbing but always sensitive, *White Women, Race Matters* courageously explores the contemporary experience of whiteness among ordinary American women and politically progressive American women. Here is whiteness as something assumed and learned and naturalized, even among anti-racists. And here is an author who is conscious of her own struggles to avoid naturalizing "race" while documenting how the women she spent hours interviewing experience it nonetheless. A book well worth reading.' - *Virginia Dominguez*

Gender, Racism, Ethnicity series
1993:
Hb: 0-415-10510-2: **£40.00** Pb: 0-415-10511-0: **£13.99**

Routledge titles are available from good bookshops or can be ordered direct from our Customer Hotline on **01264 342923.**

For more information please contact Dominic Edwardes at Routledge, 11 New Fetter Lane, London, EC4P 4EE. Tel: **0171 842 2053** or E-mail **info@routledge.com**

The Routledge catalogue is available on the Internet by accessing **http://www.routledge.com/routledge.html**

ROUTLEDGE
Women's Studies

Lesbian Studies
SETTING AN AGENDA
Tamsin Wilton

Promotes Lesbian studies as an academic and political approach to both gender and the erotic and clarifies the damaging influence of heterosexism across a range of disciplines.

August 1995:
Hb: 0-415-08655-8: **£40.00** Pb: 0-415-08656-6:**£12.99**

Reconstructing Womanhood, Reconstructing Feminism
WRITINGS ON BLACK WOMEN
Edited by **Delia Jarrett-Macauley**

' ... a unique contribution to black feminist debate and a demonstration of the strengths of feminist theory grounded in experience.' - *Sheila Rowbotham, World Institute for Development Economics Research*

November 1995:
Hb: 0-415-11648-1: **£37.50** Pb: 0-415-11649-X:**£12.99**

New in Paperback
Women Against Slavery
THE BRITISH CAMPAIGNS, 1780-1870
Clare Midgley

The first full study of women's participation in the British anti-slavery movement. It explores women's distinctive contributions and shows how these were vital in shaping successive stages of the abolitionist campaign.

May 1995: illus.14 illustrations
Pb: 0-415-12708-4: **£12.99**

Sexy Bodies
THE STRANGE CARNALITIES OF FEMINISM
Edited by **Elizabeth Grosz** and **Elspeth Probyn**

Through an examination of a variety of cultural forms and texts including the fiction of Jeanette Winterson and the body of Elizabeth Taylor, Sexy Bodies investigates the production of sexual bodies, sexual practices and sexualities.

July 1995:
Hb: 0-415-09802-5: **£40.00** Pb: 0-415-09803-3:**£12.99**

The Spivak Reader
Edited by **Donna Landry** and **George MacLean**

Among the foremost feminist critics to have emerged over the last fifteen years, Gayatri Spivak has relentlessly challenged established approaches to literary and cultural studies. This reader brings together the most salient readings of trends in Marxism, feminism and poststructuralism.

September 1995:
Hb: 0-415-91000-5: **£40.00** Pb: 0-415-91001-3:**£12.99**

New in Paperback
Women and Property in Early Modern England
Amy Louise Erickson

'**An impressive study.**' - *Germaine Greer, The Guardian*
'**Extremely stimulating.**' - *Antonia Fraser, The Times*
'**... well written: clear, urbane, often elegant and sometimes spiced with a rather sharp but never intrusive wit ... a remarkable achievement.**' - *Ralph Houlbrooke, University of Reading*

July 1995:
Pb: 0-415-13340-8: **£14.99**